# THE

---

# RETROGRADE

---

## GUIDEBOOK

An All-in-One Astrology Guide to the Cycles
of Planetary Retrograde and How They Affect
Your Emotions, Decisions, and Relationships

### JENNIFER BILLOCK

ULYSSES
PRESS

Published by:
Ulysses Press
PO Box 3440
Berkeley, CA 94703
www.ulyssespress.com

ISBN: 978-1-64604-542-6
Library of Congress Control Number: 2023938339

Printed in the United States
10 9 8 7 6 5 4 3

Acquisitions editor: Claire Sielaff
Managing editor: Claire Chun
Project editor: Paulina Maurovich
Editor: Renee Rutledge
Proofreader: Beret Olsen
Front cover design: Ashley Prine
Interior design and layout: Jake Flaherty Design
Production: Winnie Liu, Yesenia Garcia-Lopez

NOTE TO READERS: This book has been written and published strictly for informational and educational purposes only. It is not intended to serve as medical advice or to be any form of medical treatment. You should always consult your physician before altering or changing any aspect of your medical treatment and/or undertaking a diet regimen, including the guidelines as described in this book. Do not stop or change any prescription medications without the guidance and advice of your physician. Any use of the information in this book is made on the reader's good judgment after consulting with his or her physician and is the reader's sole responsibility. This book is not intended to diagnose or treat any medical condition and is not a substitute for a physician. This book is independently authored and published and no sponsorship or endorsement of this book by, and no affiliation with, any trademarked brands or other products mentioned within is claimed or suggested. All trademarks that appear in ingredient lists and elsewhere in this book belong to their respective owners and are used here for informational purposes only. The author and publisher encourage readers to patronize the brands mentioned in this book.

# CONTENTS

INTRODUCTION. . . . . . . . . . . . . . . . . . . . . . . . . . . . . .1

## SECTION I: RETROGRADE 101

CHAPTER 1
THE ASTRONOMICAL SCIENCE OF RETROGRADES. . . . . . . . . . . . 4

CHAPTER 2
THE ASTROLOGICAL SCIENCE OF RETROGRADES . . . . . . . . . . . . 7

CHAPTER 3
EARTH AND THE LUMINARIES. . . . . . . . . . . . . . . . . . . . .17

CHAPTER 4
OTHER FACTORS THAT MAY AFFECT RETROGRADES. . . . . . . . . . 21

## SECTION II: PLANET-BY-PLANET RETROGRADE GUIDE

CHAPTER 5
MERCURY. . . . . . . . . . . . . . . . . . . . . . . . . . . . . . . 48
Confusion to Clarity . . . . . . . . . . . . . . . . . . . . . . . . . . .62

CHAPTER 6
VENUS . . . . . . . . . . . . . . . . . . . . . . . . . . . . . . . 64
Letters for Self-Love, Current Love, and Past Love . . . . . . . . . . . . .69

CHAPTER 7
MARS. . . . . . . . . . . . . . . . . . . . . . . . . . . . . . . .71
Where I've Been, Where I'm Going . . . . . . . . . . . . . . . . . . . . 76

CHAPTER 8
JUPITER . . . . . . . . . . . . . . . . . . . . . . . . . . . . . . 78
Expand Your Mind Crystal Grid . . . . . . . . . . . . . . . . . . . . 81

CHAPTER 9
SATURN . . . . . . . . . . . . . . . . . . . . . . . . . . . . . . 83
Stomping Out Bad Habits . . . . . . . . . . . . . . . . . . . 86

**CHAPTER 10**
## URANUS. . . . . . . . . . . . . . . . . . . . . . . . . . . . . . . 88
Creative IndividualiTEA . . . . . . . . . . . . . . . . . . . . . . 91

**CHAPTER 11**
## NEPTUNE . . . . . . . . . . . . . . . . . . . . . . . . . . . . . 93
Intuitive Self-Hypnosis . . . . . . . . . . . . . . . . . . . . . . .96

**CHAPTER 12**
## WHAT ABOUT PLUTO? . . . . . . . . . . . . . . . . . . . .98
Embracing Your Shadow Self. . . . . . . . . . . . . . . . . .102

**CHAPTER 13**
## CHIRON WHO? . . . . . . . . . . . . . . . . . . . . . . . . . 104
Healing Ritual Bath . . . . . . . . . . . . . . . . . . . . . . . .108

**CHAPTER 14**
## RETROGRADE WRAP-UP. . . . . . . . . . . . . . . . . . .110

# SECTION III: RETROGRADE CALENDARS

**CHAPTER 15**
## RETROGRADE CALENDARS THROUGH 2030. . . . . . . . . . . . . . .114

# SECTION IV: RESOURCES
## GLOSSARY . . . . . . . . . . . . . . . . . . . . . . . . . . . 124
Websites . . . . . . . . . . . . . . . . . . . . . . . . . . . . . 127
Books . . . . . . . . . . . . . . . . . . . . . . . . . . . . . . . 127
Podcasts. . . . . . . . . . . . . . . . . . . . . . . . . . . . . .128
Apps . . . . . . . . . . . . . . . . . . . . . . . . . . . . . . . .128
Schools . . . . . . . . . . . . . . . . . . . . . . . . . . . . . .129
Organizations . . . . . . . . . . . . . . . . . . . . . . . . . . .129
Astrologers from This Book . . . . . . . . . . . . . . . . . . .129

## ABOUT THE AUTHOR . . . . . . . . . . . . . . . . . . . .131

# INTRODUCTION

I t's inevitable to have a bad day, week, or month, when nothing is going right and it feels like everything is falling apart. When this happens, you vent to some friends, and suddenly someone says, "Mercury must be in retrograde!" A knowing, sympathetic nod runs through the group.

Take a moment to ask yourself, though: Is Mercury *actually* retrograde right now? Do you know what really happens when it is? And what is retrograde anyway? Not many people know, but the buzzword comes up almost daily.

In truth, it seems like Mercury retrograde is more of an excuse than a reality these days. Sure, it can be a tumultuous time when it does happen, but your frustrations aren't always Mercury's fault. Mercury rules communication, so it makes sense that we're the most vocal about our frustrations when the planet retrogrades. The reality is that every planet except Earth goes retrograde at some point, and each planet has its own accompanying bundle of joys and pain points.

This book aims to take the mystery out of planetary retrogrades. It provides an overview of what retrograde means astrologically and the basic principles, then puts that overview to work with a breakdown of every retrograde throughout the year. You'll learn every planetary retrograde's function and effects and why three main celestial bodies, the Earth, sun, and moon, don't ever go into retrograde. And if you've ever wondered what happens when a lunar or solar eclipse coincides with a retrograde, this book will answer that question.

Personally, I've been interested in astrology and the effect it has on our lives since I was small. As I grew up and learned to fully embrace my Leo self, that interest only expanded. I began looking to retrogrades to see how they affected things happening in my life, and the connections—like my computer crashing when Mercury was retrograde—were too on point to ignore. I've brought all that experience into this book, plus extensive research and interviews with 12 full-time astrologers who could shed light on retrograde aspects I hadn't learned yet.

Along with providing general information about each retrograde, this guidebook explains how it will affect you as an individual and what that looks like from a practical perspective. The book also includes ways to manage and cope with the stress that comes with retrogrades. Plus, you'll learn how to maximize the benefits of each one so the planets essentially work on your behalf to improve your life.

To help you with future retrogrades, you'll also find calendars through 2030. These calendars include the dates each planet goes into and out of retrograde, and the astrological signs each planet is leaving and entering. Don't get caught unawares—with all the information this guidebook arms you with, you'll never fear a retrograde again.

# SECTION I

## RETROGRADE 101

# Chapter 1

# THE ASTRONOMICAL SCIENCE OF RETROGRADES

At the most basic level, planetary retrogrades are astronomical phenomena. Every planet has its own orbit around the sun. So, if we were to look at it in the night sky, each planet would appear to be moving from right to left, which is called *direct* movement or a *direct transit*. But sometimes—when, how often, and how long all depending on each planet's respective orbit—the planet would appear to go backward, from left to right. That's called a retrograde transit.

Retrogrades happen when a planet appears to be moving in the opposite direction of its typical path, or in another direction from all the other planets in the solar system, when viewed from Earth and followed over time. It's ultimately an optical illusion; the planet's orbit hasn't actually changed, it's just a matter of how we're viewing the differences in orbit compared to our humble home.

"Understand that retrogrades as we see them are an optical illusion based on our position on Earth relative to the position of that planet and the position of the sun," says Brian Allemana, founder of Soulrise Astrology, a blog and business offering astrological readings and salons. "It's like when you're in a train. Two trains are pulling out of a station, one starts to speed up, and for a moment it looks like the other is going backward. It's that kind of optical illusion, though it's not a perfect analogy."

Think about it this way: If you were watching a planet orbit around the sun from Earth, assuming you could see the planet clearly the entire time, you wouldn't really see a circle. You'd see it go one way, and then double back the way it came. It would look like it was going backward.

A planetary retrograde is a multipart experience. As a planet's orbit begins to pass Earth's, the planet enters what's called a shadow period. First, the planet, say Mars, enters the pre-shadow period, and as its orbit crosses Earth's, it looks at first like Mars totally stops (station retrograde); then Mars appears to go backward in the sky, retracing the span of the shadow period in a retrograde motion. After Mars hits the beginning of the shadow period, it appears to stop again (station direct) and then starts to move forward, covering that same span (a post-shadow period) for a third time. So Mars appears to go forward, then backward, then forward again. And that's a retrograde.

And remember that each planet retrogrades according to its own orbit. Some years, a planet may not retrograde at all. See the charts at the end of this book for examples. With Mars, we typically see its retrograde motion every other year. That's because Mars's orbit is wider and about twice as long as Earth's, so Mars has a full revolution around the sun once every two Earth years. Mercury, on the other hand, orbits the sun in 88 days, so we see it retrograde more often.

Astronomically, retrogrades don't mean all that much. They're just the regular movement of the planets in orbit. A *Discovery* article from September 2022, "Six Planets Are Retrograde, What Does That Mean for You?"[1] sums up astronomers' feelings on the topic pretty well: "It means nothing at all. One planet moving in retrograde

---

1   Paul M. Sutter, "Six Planets Are Retrograde, What Does That Mean for You?," Discovery.com, September 27, 2022, https://www.discovery.com/space/six-planet-retrograde.

doesn't mean anything either—it's literally just a planet moving in its orbit, doing the same thing it's been doing for the past four and a half billion years."

Many people place heightened importance on multiple retrogrades happening at once, saying that affects peoples' lives more than a single retrograde would, but astronomers aren't buying that either. From an astronomical point of view, it's just an inevitability of the perpetual motion of the planets and their different speeds. If planets are rotating through the galaxy at different speeds, it makes sense several could be retrograde at once. Multiple retrogrades are not magical or impactful to astronomers, who are quick to point out that this has happened for eons, and you—not retrogrades—are in control of your own life.

## Chapter 2

# THE ASTROLOGICAL SCIENCE OF RETROGRADES

While astronomy is a study of the stars, planets, and their motions, astrology is a bit different. It's still a study of the stars, planets, and their motions, but instead focuses on how those celestial bodies and their placement affect us—both from birth, like with your zodiac sign, and throughout the years of our lives.

Astrologically, each retrograde period has a meaning. The shadow periods are integral for working through that meaning.

"The pre-shadow phase will usually come with a hint of a situation, something that needs attention or adjustment," says Charly King, the astrology host for NOW! Radio's *Bob & Sheri Show*, a weekly syndicated radio feature. "Then, during the retrograde itself, this matter becomes obvious and active. The post-shadow phase tends to come with a need to debrief and realign the actions."

Think of a retrograde periods like a budding relationship. In the pre-shadow period, you realize you have a crush on someone. In the retrograde period, you go on a date with them. In the post-shadow period, you think about how the date went and consider if you'll work out together. The process goes from thought, to experience, to aftereffects.

It's a bit of a misconception that you won't feel a retrograde outside of the planet's actual retrograde transit. The astrological truth is that you begin to feel it a week or two before and still feel it for a week or two after. You feel those shadow periods, even if they're not completely obvious.

Astrologer KJ Atlas, who has seven retrograde planets in her birth chart (which some astrologers believe could make life quite a bit more difficult for someone), says, "The intensity of the retrograde will start to lessen after the retrograde, and it will build up before the retrograde. This is why the exact dates of the beginning and end of retrogrades should be viewed as approximate. You're not going to automatically *not* feel the retrograde the day after it is over. The shadow period will lighten up over the coming days and weeks after a cycle and will give you time to recalibrate."

For example, when Mercury retrograde is on the way, we might notice we've become more sensitive to the news we're reading each day (especially since Mercury rules communication, among other things). During the retrograde period itself, it may be too much to even look at the news. Then, when Mercury eases out of the retrograde cycle, we may slowly pick back up the habit of reading the daily paper.

That being said, though, astrologers are split on which part of the retrograde cycle we feel most intensely. Andi Javor, astrologer and founder of Mystic Sandwich, a company that provides astrological readings, believes the stations are the most intense times, when the crossing planet is just sitting there, barely moving at all, assaulting us with its energy. King agrees, relating the stations to something like crescendos in a musical score.

"In the approach to the peak, as the pre-shadow phase moves closer to the retrograde, intensification, like the crescendo in music, can be expected," King says, "and even a physical or literal event, like the breaking of electronics or the arrival of legal documents during the Mercury retrograde pre-shadow. The post-shadow phase is more reflective, intellectual, and passive, [for] assimilating the lessons learned."

Mashi Salomon, astrologer and owner at Light and Lavender, a Colorado-based company providing astrology readings and energy work, suggests the post-shadow period is the most important time of the retrograde, however. She says that sometimes, we don't even know we are in a retrograde until it's over and we're left to pick up the pieces from whatever craziness happened during the transit.

It makes sense if you think about it. A retrograde is an illusion because the planet isn't really going backward. And if you're in an illusion—like in a house of mirrors—it's pretty difficult to know exactly what's going on. Once you get out of it, when the planet heads to the post-shadow period, you're left wondering exactly what happened and dealing with the aftereffects.

Robert Wilkinson, author and founder of the long-running blog *Aquarius Papers*, doesn't necessarily agree. For him, the post-shadow period is the easiest, because we've already been through that transit twice.

"By the third pass, we should already have some expertise in understanding what the whole thing was about in the house or houses where it happened," he says. "We got three different views of whatever it was that span of our experience was about. We should already have some understanding of it because we've experienced it twice."

Throughout history, though, retrogrades have generally been categorized as good or bad overall, with no nuance—at least not one that's commonly known.

Back in the medieval era, astrologers were revered and respected scholars who advised on everything from health to religion. They were also considered quite skilled in predicting the outcomes of battles. So a battle would begin, and they'd draw up a star map for each side. If they saw a retrograde in the chart on a particular side, it wasn't a great sign. They would say that side was not engaged in the rules of the game and was going against the rules. Clearly, Western civilization has a long history of considering retrogrades to be bad.

Vedic astrology is Hindu astrology that looks at the current positions of the constellations, rather than where they sit in the fixed, Western astrological system that this book refers to. Vedic astrology also focuses less on our psychology and more on our individual karma. In that system, retrogrades are considered a strength, mainly because a planet is brighter in the sky when it's retrograde. In Sanskrit, Vedic astrology is called *jyotiṣa*—which roughly translates to "light" or "heavenly body." When a planet appears brighter in the sky, it's a more potent planet.

The opposing views are a great example of the duality of retrogrades. On the surface, they can seem like a bad thing. But when you look a little closer, they're actually a positive because they enable us to better understand the behavioral, spiritual, and psychological effects of the celestial illusion.

"Life is a series of making choices to replace unhealthy responses with healthy responses," Wilkinson says. "Eventually, we create really constructive and positive karmic patterns. Then, whether it's direct [when a planet appears to be stopped in the sky] or retrograde, no matter what sign it's in, we are getting the lessons we're supposed to get, and we are becoming an expert in our use of [that] energy.... There is then no sign position which paralyzes us or which leads us to an unhealthy expression. We can actually understand, through the retrograde review and reflection and reconsideration process, how we want to express things."

# Handling Retrogrades Like a Champ

OK, first things first. Repeat after me:

*No matter what's in retrograde, it's not the end of the world. It is not the end of the world.*

Good.

We've been through *so many* retrograde periods already. And we will live through so many more. Worrying that everything is suddenly going to be this huge disaster is not really worth your time.

Angelica Kurtz, astrologer and founder of astrology business and blog *Astro Obscura*, suggests bracing for the impact of planetary retrogrades. And sure, that sounds a little rough. But trust me, it's not. Just be prepared for what might happen, or what might be more likely to happen.

"Not to make it out to be this big deal or anything, but people tend to realize during retrogrades that something is amiss," she says. "You know, they're losing their car keys. Technology isn't working. Something is off. And then they tend to look at the internet to see what's going on. Oh, Mercury's in retrograde."

But you can avoid that entire issue of not knowing what's going on just by checking in advance to see what energy is coming and figuring out how it might affect you. Is it Venus? Be prepared for relationship stresses. Mercury? Get ready for communication problems, and don't make any major appointments. Mars? Watch your temper! And don't decide on anything big if you have your own business—you'll want to wait until later, when you're in a clearer headspace and not at risk of making rash decisions.

Rowan Oliver, astrologer and founder of astrological consulting business StarScribe Astrology, agrees. They suggest not taking any decisive action during a retrograde; instead, think about what needs to change and really be intentional about those thoughts. If you need to make a big life decision during a retrograde, you shouldn't shy away from it. Just take some extra time to deliberate on it.

"You can't just be like, 'I'm going to put off signing this lease because Mercury is retrograde, but my other lease is ending and I need to move somewhere,'" Oliver says.

Just be aware that decisions you make during retrogrades are malleable. The outcome may be more likely to change or get reconfigured in the future. Be open to that happening. Sure, not everything's going to be ideal during a retrograde period. But if you're intentional with your thoughts and actions, you can move from a place of "Oh no, what do I do?" to "All right, some things are in motion that I can't control. How do I work with that?"

Astrologer and life coach Julia Mihas thinks about it as astrological weather. Is a planet moving direct? That's like it being sunny. If it's retrograde, that's like rain. It's up to you whether you bring an umbrella. And if you've looked at the weather forecast or taken a step outside to see the clouds rolling in, you're better prepared for that incoming storm.

One of the first lines of defense for making sure you're able to easily handle retrograde periods, says Deborah Norton of Deborah Norton Astrology, a company offering astrological readings, is to figure out your own personal astrology. Get your birth chart done so you can see where all your retrogrades were when you were born and what houses and other planets they aligned with. That basic knowledge will take you pretty far in feeling more comfortable during retrograde periods. We'll learn about getting your birth chart done—and what it means for you if you have retrogrades in your chart—in Chapter 4.

"I think our culture is not aligned with the energies that are swirling around us all the time," Norton says. "And so, that's why we're a little out of whack, why there's so much depression, anxiety, and all of that;

it's because we're not living in harmony and consciousness with the energies that are influencing us."

Retrogrades are the natural ebb and flow of life, Norton says, comparing them to inhaling and exhaling. When we exhale, we move forward. But sometimes we forget to inhale. And that's what retrogrades are there for. They're gifts, she says, that allows us a moment of rest, pause, and reflection. And if you aren't prepared with your own birth chart to see that moment coming, you'll react to it a little differently. Not to say that your birth chart can predict oncoming retrogrades (we've got retrograde dates through 2030 at the end of the book for that), but your birth chart will show you where your own personal retrogrades are. And that's information that may make you react a bit differently to the recurrent retrogrades you'll experience throughout the years.

"We often don't take it as [a rest] because we don't understand it," Norton says. "So we get stressed out and we get anxious when we don't understand why the energy doesn't feel normal, when what we're used to is forward motion."

# Retrograde Reflection

At the end of every retrograde period, it's smart to take stock of how it went. Personally, I recommend a retrograde journal where you track all the retrogrades and their effects on you and your life. But if you're not a journaler, try something else that fits your personality more. Maybe you could make a retrograde-themed art piece or record yourself speaking about how everything went. Consider the following questions as your write, create, or narrate:

1. Think about how you thought the retrograde would go, and how it was different from what you expected. Was it scary?

2. Did something hidden come to the surface?

3. Were you faced with something that had been previously resolved?

If you make these observations, you'll be able to reference your notes later on. That way, you don't run into the same issues you encountered during the previous retrograde.

"Be wary of popular astrological tropes about retrogrades that make it sound like they're just totally bad, that you should just hide in your closet and never come out until the retrograde's over," Allemana says. "That's not the right approach to retrogrades. If you are in a fender bender during Mercury retrograde or you have some sort of problem that manifests that you're able to see really matches the retrograde you're going through, take it inward. Don't judge it as something terrible, or judge yourself. Find the meaning in it for yourself. There's always a meaning there and you can always derive some value from that. Don't be afraid of retrogrades. Meet them with the same curiosity and openness and respect for life that you would like to have yourself met with."

Javor agrees and says that astrology should be a collaborative experience between us and the heavens.

"See yourself as a participant in the cosmos rather than seeing astrology as something that happens to us that is just going to predict how things unfold," she says. "If we perceive it as like we're cooperating with or collaborating with or working with these energies, then there's a lot more opportunity and creativity and possibility."

Think about how you can best work with the planets. What can they teach you and what can you observe from the retrograde period? Then take that knowledge with you as you move forward to tackle future retrogrades.

# It's Not You, It's the Retrograde—Or Not

So, last week was terrible. I lost my house keys in the store and couldn't find my car in the parking lot. Then, when I finally recovered my keys and got in the car, my phone wouldn't connect to the Bluetooth and I had to call my husband using my phone *like regular*. And THEN, my husband and I got in a fight about who took the garbage out last time, and I got so mad that I hung up on him. *Something has to be in retrograde.* There's no way I would have done any of that if I had any control over the situation. Right?

Well, actually, wrong.

This is one of modern society's biggest misconceptions about retrogrades. Sure, there may be circumstances and influences outside your control happening with the retrograde. But, no matter what the planets are doing, they're not forcing you to do anything or making you act outside your own free will. You're probably just…whining.

"The planets don't make anything happen," Wilkinson says. "We're all under countless retrograde influences, whether we're acting, reacting, or being acted upon."

Oliver agrees, noting that a lot of times, when people blame things on retrogrades, they're really just trying to make an excuse for an intentional action or trying to use the retrograde period as a cop-out.

It is possible, though, that the retrograde has created a situation that makes all these things—fighting, being careless with your belongings, hanging up on someone—a little bit more likely to happen.

"A retrograde will never compel you to act a certain way," King says. "It may, however, create certain environmental dynamics that require a different speed."

So, if you have a tough relationship with a friend or family member, a retrograde isn't going to force you to hang up on them during a particularly frustrating conversation. But it may create an environment where communication is a bit more difficult. And if you don't alter your communication style during that period, things can get over-blown or out of control.

"Each planet shows us a part of our personality," Wilkinson says. "It's our job to elevate their expression to the highest level; materially, emotionally, mentally, and spiritually across the personal, interpersonal, and transpersonal dimensions of human existence."

That means taking the time to look at what each planet represents and considering how it might affect you or your life during a retrograde. Let's use Saturn as an example. The planet represents discipline and structure. How do you handle discipline personally? Do you have trouble staying on task? That's something to think about before Saturn retrogrades. You'll also want to consider how you react to discipline from an interpersonal perspective—like maybe you don't take it well when someone wants to impose rules on you.

When you're armed with all this information about a planet's function and how you interact with it, you'll be able to pay more attention to your attitude during the retrograde. And if you do that enough, your attitude will change on a transpersonal—or subconscious—level.

# Chapter 3

# EARTH AND THE LUMINARIES

At this point, you might be asking: What about Earth? Do *we* go retrograde? And then you might try to run backward, or in a direction you're not used to, just to see what happens, and you could fall, and it would be pretty much a big old mess.

OK, well probably not, but the idea is pretty funny if you think about it.

In technical terms, yes, the Earth goes retrograde. You just need to be on another planet to see it. Since we don't see our own planet moving through space from a distance (unless you're an astronaut), there's no way for us to see if our transit looks backward. If we could, that would cause a whole different heap of problems. So while Earth technically does retrograde, it doesn't for us, nor is it considered something that retrogrades in the astrological sense. Remember that all retrograde cycles are an optical illusion based on how we see each planet's movement *from Earth*.

The other two celestial bodies that don't ever retrograde are called luminaries. They are the sun and the moon, and both are considered planets in astrology.

# The Sun

The sun doesn't retrograde because it doesn't move.

I hear you astronomy people in the back shouting that it does, so let's get this out of the way now. Technically, yes, the sun moves. It spins around its axis, but remember that the sun is made up of gas and plasma, so it has no solid surface. The gas and plasma rotate, but they move faster around the sun's equator than at the poles. That rotation is similar to the outer planets in our solar system—Jupiter, Saturn, Uranus, and Neptune—which also have a gas construction. The California Institute of Technology notes that at its equator, the sun has a full rotation once every 24 days. At the poles, it's once every 35 days.[2]

The sun also orbits around the center of the Milky Way, but it takes everything in our solar system with it when it goes. Right now, as you're reading this, we're moving at about 450,000 miles per hour along with the sun.

That all being said, Earth orbits around the sun. So to us, the sun is stationary. That means that it won't retrograde because its orbit won't pass ours, so the whole retrograde optical illusion cannot take place.

# The Moon

For a planet to have a retrograde period, it needs to orbit around the sun. And yes, while the moon does orbit around the sun, it does so as part of *our* orbit. The moon orbits around us while we orbit around the sun, so it always appears to be moving direct. Remember, moving directly means moving east to west, or in a right-to-left direction through the sky.

---

2  "Does the Sun Spin?," Cool Cosmos, last accessed July 6, 2023, https://coolcosmos.ipac .caltech.edu/ask/9-Does-the-Sun-spin.

# Eclipses

According to some astrologers, the sun and moon can retrograde—in a way. That's where eclipses come in. Eclipses have their own astrological effect. They're big moments in our energetic lives.

Solar eclipses represent new and unexpected experiences, those that come to us by way of a sudden life event that's out of our control. And we need to act quickly to resolve whatever that life event is. Think of it as a random event, like suddenly getting a new project at work that requires you to quickly wrap up what you had been working on beforehand.

Lunar eclipses, on the other hand, represent the culmination, or end, of something. They start a cycle of clearing things out of our lives. An example would be realizing you need to break up with someone, and then starting the breakup process.

Think of it this way: if a solar eclipse is getting fired from your job, a lunar eclipse is resigning from your job. Both are major events that move you past complacency and put you on a new track to personal growth.

"I kind of look at eclipses as being retrograde periods for the sun and moon," Mihas says. "They act in a similar way….The sun and moon are the only astrological 'planets' that don't go retrograde, but their eclipse seasons [have] some similarities in the behavior."

She notes that the effects can be more intense depending on what sign the eclipse is happening in, as well as the eclipse's saros cycle. According to Mihas, eclipses run in families that go in 18-year cycles, with eclipses happening in the same spots astrologically within those cycles. The cycles string together into saros series that can last thousands of years.

And, you can find historical events that connect to the saros cycles. One example is a financial depression. Astrologer and author Celeste

Teal predicted 2020 would be a terrible time for the world financially because the eclipses of that year were in the same eclipse family—called Solar Saros 127—as the ones from the Great Depression. We were in Solar Saros 127 when the stock market crashed in 1857 in the US and Europe; when the stock market crashed in 1893; when the stock market crashed and the Great Depression began in 1929; and when the stock market crashed and 9/11 happened in 2001. Solar Saros 127 was set to begin again in July 2019, and look what happened: Covid-19 emerged and everyone's finances went wild.

Mihas also ties solar eclipses to some other major world events. She notes that Donald Trump's birth chart shows he was born during an eclipse. And shortly before the January 6 insurrection, another eclipse hit his natal eclipse spot within a couple of degrees.

"It was just bananas," she says. "[Eclipses are] fascinating for understanding world events. And again, like a retrograde, there's something about [eclipses] not playing by the rules of the game, which is why I compare sun and moon eclipses to retrograde planets."

# Chapter 4

# OTHER FACTORS THAT MAY AFFECT RETROGRADES

Astrology is all about energy and the planets giving off that energy. In your own personal astrological reading, any number of things can affect how you react and interact with that planetary energy, such as what phase the moon is in and what house your personal ruling planets were in at the time of your birth.

It makes sense to deduce that anything affecting personal astrology will also affect retrogrades and how we handle them. But that's not always the case. Because retrograde motion is tied to the planets and not to you personally, some things—like nodes, for example, which are mathematical points marking the spot in the sky where the sun and moon pass one another as seen from Earth—won't have much of an impact.

Keep reading to find out what astrological items might affect retrograde energy, and how.

# Birth Charts

Birth charts are a map of what the planets looked like in the astrological sky at the exact moment you were born. It's a circular chart representing 24 hours, broken into 12 sections, each with a ruling zodiac sign and house.

A house, which is a section of the chart that represents a personality trait (you'll learn more about houses later in this chapter), covers about two hours in the chart. Each planet in your chart is represented by a symbol, and that planet will be plotted on your birth chart according to what zodiac sign and house it was passing through at the time you were born.

For example, I was born with Venus in Virgo, which is the sixth house—the house that represents routines. Your chart will also show you what degree each planet was at when you were born. Degrees mark each segment of movement a planet makes around the sky, and each zodiac sign and its house occupies 30 degrees. So for me, Venus was in Virgo at 7 degrees. (Don't worry if that's a little confusing. You'll learn more about degrees in the Degree Theory section later in this chapter.) Not every house and zodiac in your birth chart will have a planet in it, so don't be alarmed if you notice that.

A natal retrograde is when one of the planets was retrograde during the day and time you were born. You can gather this information from your birth chart; you'll need your exact date and time of birth to get one. Once you have that information, you can go online to a site like CafeAstrology.com, plug in your birthdate and time, and the chart will be generated for you. Websites to create your chart are easily found and generally free to use. The retrograde planet will be marked with a little "R" or some other symbol, depending on the website that made your chart.

At first glance, a retrograde in your birth chart might be alarming, like it's a bad thing. But it's not and shouldn't be considered as such.

"Retrograde doesn't condemn us to some kind of malfunction," Wilkinson says. "That's like people saying, 'If I don't have a planet in the house then that means that house is empty and it's not important,' which is insane. Because all 12 sectors of our life are important. 'Oh, gee, my fifth house [the house that represents creativity] doesn't have any planets, so therefore I have no creativity.' I've actually heard people tell me that. I say that's crazy. That doesn't mean no creativity. It just merely means that you're searching for that particular sign's expression of creativity."

The retrograde planets in your birth chart have a fairly simple effect on you later in life. They might make it easier for you to deal with those specific planetary retrogrades. You've essentially been dealing with that energy your entire life, which means you have more practice with it.

"When you're born during a retrograde, it's almost like you live in that retrograde mindset," Kurtz says, "which can make things a little trickier when you're younger because you're almost living at a different speed from everybody else."

Using Mercury retrograde as an example, Kurtz notes seeing a pattern of readings in which customers who have Mercury retrograde in their birth chart tend to have more issues with focus and concentration throughout life.

"When Mercury retrograde comes around again, it's almost as if the rest of the world is meeting their brain speed," she says. "Everybody else is freaking out because, 'Oh my God, this is different from the norm, and we don't know how to handle it.' And then the people who have Mercury retrograde natally are just like, 'Now you're all on my level.' So, it does tend to make it a little difficult when they're growing up, and it's this extra challenge that they need to work through. But because they've been working with that challenge, they almost become better at those planets."

Atlas agrees.

"Some say that retrograde periods are 'superpower' periods for retrograde people, and you might feel more inspired," she says.

Even so, that doesn't mean you should be going out and making all sorts of decisions that involve other people, like launching group projects, signing contracts, or holding important meetings. Not everyone will be on your same wavelength—they might not have your particular retrograde "superpower." Find ways to enjoy that leg up you've got on the retrograde period on your own.

It's important to remember that just because a retrograde period may be easier for you, that doesn't mean it's going to be easy for everyone. We're all different. Again, let's use Mercury retrograde as an example. That particular transit can make travel a mess, with delayed flights, lost bags, seat confusion, and other things along those lines. But people born with a natal Mercury retrograde may actually enjoy the challenge or deal with it better than others. Their natal retrograde acts in their favor.

"I tell them, just because you're doing well doesn't mean anybody else is," astrologer Susan Levitt says. "You have Mercury retrograde and it's good for you; great. I understand that. But that's not most people."

Besides, someone having a natal retrograde doesn't necessarily mean they're going to make the right choices, or the choices that are easier for them, during the retrograde period. They may have been attuned to that energy since birth, but they can still make mistakes.

Some astrologers, like Salomon, believe that you're attuned to the specific energy of your natal retrograde because that planet was an issue for you even before this life.

"Retrogrades in a planet means there was a struggle in a past life with that planet's energy," she says. "Part of your mission in this world is to fix and focus on that energy. So it's not something to run away from. …It's that planet basically knocking on your door being like, 'Hey, we didn't fix or deal with or heal this energy in a past life,' and so it shows up as something that we can work on in this life."

That's why it's important to work with your natal retrograde energy instead of against it. And if you get your birth chart done, you'll be able to see those retrogrades and learn what configuration you're working with exactly, allowing you to make the best choices and decisions possible.

Wilkinson feels similarly, noting that it's our goal to see our personal planets through to completion on a karmic scale.

"The problem isn't the malfunction of the planet, not in what sign it's in, not in who we are, because we are eternals having a human experience," he says. "The chart shows us our divinity and it shows us our worldly side, and we have to somehow integrate those two because ultimately, we're here to perfect every one of our planets so that we can live as our highest self and fulfill our purpose for being here."

That being said, retrogrades in your natally retrograde planet won't always be a cakewalk. If you're still struggling with the themes of that retrograde, they're going to be a little bit more intensely in your face. And that's not something you should hide from. Instead, it's a sign you need to work on the issues more.

"That's sort of how those retrogrades show up in the birth chart," Oliver says. "It takes longer for the lessons of communication, or love and beauty in relationships, or anger and drive and activity to really show up for you in a way that is constructive and a way that you can actually do things with. A lot of the time it starts out as something that's really difficult for you to get a grasp on until later in life."

There's also something called a progressed chart, which applies the concept that your natal energy evolves and changes along with you, leading to slight differences in how your birth chart is manifested in your life.

In a progressed chart, each year you've been alive equals a day on the birth chart. So you start with your natal chart (which still applies to you!) and move the birth date forward a day for each year of your age. Say you were born in Chicago at 2 p.m. on May 1, 1990, and you want to see how your chart changed when you were 10. You would move your birth date to May 11 (remember, one year is one day on the chart) and create a new astrological chart based on the date May 11, 1990, at 2 p.m., in Chicago.

Based on those 1990 dates, some of the planet placements have changed. On your birthday, May 1, 1990, the moon was in Leo and Venus was in Pisces. But in the progressed chart, the moon is in Sagittarius and Venus is in Aries. That means that something happened that year that made an impact on your life. For the moon placement, it was likely something related to travel, which Sagittarius represents. For Venus, it was likely a change related to courage, which Aries represents. (You'll learn more about what each zodiac sign represents later in this chapter.)

As I mentioned, your original birth chart still applies. So, the progressed chart acts as more of an overlay—like a software update on your computer. Your birth chart isn't gone, it's just enhanced with new energy.

## Moon Phases

Typically, the moon phase has no bearing on how much you feel—or don't feel—the effects of a planetary retrograde. But, where the moon is and at what phase it is in your birth chart could have an indirect effect on retrogrades for you, specifically.

"The lunar phase will have an effect over the collective and personal emotional state and emotional well-being," Kurtz says. So if you have the moon in Taurus—which has a lot to do with money and finances—during a retrograde in your birth chart, "that might be the area where you're feeling particularly bogged down by whatever planetary energy is retrograding at the time."

# Aspects

Aspects in planetary charts refer to the angle two planets are separated by, which influences the relationship between those two planets. Generally, there are two types of aspects: hard (two planets separated by an odd number of zodiac signs on the astrological chart) and soft (two planets separated by an even number of zodiac signs on the astrological chart). Hard aspects mean there's more tension between two planets, so if one of them is retrograde, it could be an especially difficult time. Soft aspects are the opposite; the two planets help each other out, so you'll have an easier time with the retrograde planet.

Astrologers and astrological charts use this basic set of aspects:

**Conjunction:** Neither hard nor soft. Planets are fewer than 10 degrees apart.

**Opposition:** Hard. Planets are 180 degrees apart.

**Trine:** Soft. Planets are 120 degrees apart.

**Square:** Hard. Planets are 90 degrees apart.

**Sextile:** Soft. Planets are 60 degrees apart.

**Semisquare:** Hard. Planets are 45 degrees apart.

**Sesquiquadrate:** Hard. Planets are 135 degrees apart.

**Semisextile:** Hard. Planets are 30 degrees apart.

**Quincunx:** Hard. Planets are 150 degrees apart.

Conjunctions are unique in astrology. Two planets in conjunction are no longer considered separate planets; instead, their energy combines into its own type of influence.

Even with just this limited information so far, you could probably pull up today's astrological chart using one of those birth chart generators I mentioned earlier and see what's retrograding and determine whether it's worse or better for you because of the aspect.

## Lunar Nodes

Lunar nodes mark the spots in the sky where the sun and moon pass each other. There are two: the north node and the south node. Connecting the two creates a natural opposition across the sky. The south node represents the past, as in past lives. Where it lands in your birth chart shows you all the stuff you've carried through to your current life, like talents and habits. The north node represents (go figure) the future and where you're going to go from this life and into future lives.

If you did your birth chart or an astrological chart for right now and saw that the lunar nodes were in retrograde, don't freak out. The lunar nodes are *always* in retrograde. Technically, they're not even planets that can go retrograde. They're just mathematical points.

## Sects

Traditional Hellenic and medieval astrology consider the astrological changes brought by time of day. This is called looking at sect, or how your natal chart is divided between night or day.

"It's a very simple technique, but I do find it quite effective," Mihas says. "It means that if you're a day birth, meaning the sun is above the horizon line, your more challenging planet is going to be Mars. If you're a night birth, so the sun below the horizon line, you're going to have more of a challenging period with Saturn."

Further, day births will have an easier time with Venus and night births will have an easier time with Jupiter. When looking at sect, the sun rules both Jupiter and Saturn, and the moon rules both Venus and

Mars. But those planets are further separated into malefic (or bad) and benefic (or good) planets. Mars and Saturn are malefic, and Jupiter and Venus are benefic. Mercury is considered a neutral planet, and no other planets are included in sect.

That goes double for retrogrades. If Mars or Saturn is retrograde, it will likely be a more vulnerable period for you than others, based on your sect. But when Venus and Jupiter retrograde, it'll likely be easier for you, based on your sect.

Keep in mind that the sect changes based on where you are in the world. So if you and someone in Beijing, China, were born at the exact same time, you'd have different sects because it would be day in one place and night in the other.

# Quantity

Some planets retrograde more often than others. (We're looking at you, Mercury.) And while that doesn't change what the retrograde means or what it affects, it could change how we react to it—hopefully. When a planet retrogrades more than once a year, we begin to get used to the energy. And maybe we'll be able to deal with it better than how we handle a planet that only retrogrades every now and then. So, by the time Mercury makes its third or fourth retrograde transit through the sky in a given year, we really should be better equipped to put the lessons we learned in previous retrogrades into action.

# Asteroids

Asteroids likely won't change the effects of a planetary retrograde, except in a couple circumstances. You'll learn about this more later in this chapter, but the asteroid belt between Mars and Jupiter separates the planets into inner and outer planets—and that classification makes a difference in whether a retrograde affects just you or everyone.

Aside from the planets, some astrologers track retrogrades of two main asteroids: Ceres (which was reclassified as a dwarf planet in 2006) and Chiron (an anomaly to which Chapter 13 is dedicated). Ceres retrogrades for about three months every year and a half. And thanks to her namesake Roman goddess, she's also called the Earth Mother, representing encouragement, nourishment, and growth. The retrograde period for Ceres can be a little gloomy for a lot of us. We may feel like we suddenly aren't getting enough support or encouragement from the people we love, or we're suddenly missing some important resources we need to survive and grow. The best way to handle this? Find a new or similar source of abundance. Maybe you lean into a friendship that doesn't often get enough attention, or you try a new fulfilling hobby. Or, you could go the easiest route and tell people you're feeling down and you need some encouragement. Your loved ones care about you, so make sure they know how you're doing!

The asteroid belt on the whole doesn't appear to have much impact on retrograde activity because it's not tied to the movement of the planets.

# Houses

An astrological chart (also called a wheel) is broken up into 12 different houses, going counterclockwise. Each represents a major part of your life, like relationships, career, or home life. When a retrograde happens, the house that planet is in at the time can change how it affects you. For example, if Mercury were retrograde in the relationships house, you could struggle to communicate with your partner. If it were to retrograde in the career house, you might encounter a computer glitch at work that stops emails from sending. Keep in mind that more than one planet can occupy a single house at once, and sometimes a house has no planets in it.

Here's the breakdown of the astrological houses and their categories, based on Carole Taylor's book *Astrology: Using the Wisdom of the Stars in Your Everyday Life.*

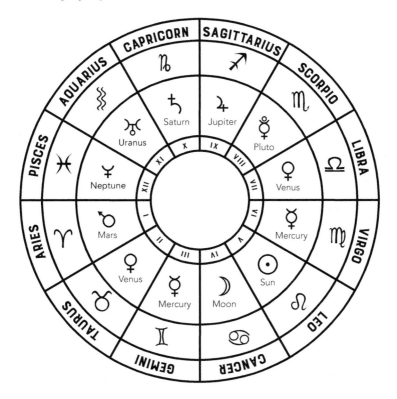

**First House:** New Beginnings. This house represents your personality, identity, and how you present yourself to the world.

**Second House:** Resources. This house represents wealth (both tangible and intangible), finances, and material possessions and desires.

**Third House:** Communication. This house represents your ideas, how you arrive at them, and how you share them with others. It also represents sibling relationships, education, and how you formed your perceptions early on in life.

**Fourth House:** Home. This house represents family (both blood and chosen), heritage, and *home* as it pertains to both the home in which you live and the place of safety within you.

**Fifth House:** Creativity. This house represents passion and play, risk-taking, creative expression, pastimes, and individuality.

**Sixth House:** Routines. This house represents the little patterns you have in day-to-day life, including the things you always do at work or home, the habits to help you maintain your health, and the way you treat others who help you.

**Seventh House:** Relationships. This house represents partnership, marriage, enemies, arguments, and your attraction to whatever you feel is missing in your own personality.

**Eighth House:** Transformation. This house represents intimacy, death, transitions, and shared belongings or finances. Things in life that are typically considered difficult or emotionally negative fall into this house.

**Ninth House:** Adventure. This house represents heading out on a journey! It could be physical or intellectual. You could be looking for meaning in life, seeking a higher level of education, taking a trip, or diving deeper into religion and ethics.

**Tenth House:** Achievement. This house represents your career and success, ambition and authority, and the way you present yourself to the public world.

**Eleventh House:** Friendships. This house represents your social networks and participation—everything you do in a group setting, from sports to council meetings. The eleventh house also represents political and social views, as well as hopes and dreams for the future.

**Twelfth House:** Service. This house represents charity, nirvana, group institutions (like a hospital or prison), sacrifice, release, and devotion.

With all the houses and their meanings in mind, you've got an arsenal of knowledge on how to approach retrogrades in each house—and how to possibly prepare for them in advance.

Salomon says retrogrades invite us to work with the energy and not against it: "It's almost a good way to fix that energy."

Retrogrades in the houses are like having a car with a weak transmission. You know that you need to keep that car up-to-date with fluid changes, repairs, and maintenance. You're aware of what hurdles you may experience and can prepare for them. It's the same with houses. If you know what the house represents and can see that a retrograde is coming up in that house, you'll be better prepared to meet the challenge when it happens.

Each house has a ruling planet and zodiac sign (a constellation that the sun passes through in that house) as well. Zodiac signs for retrogrades note what part of the astrological wheel the planet is in when it transits through.

When a planet retrogrades in its ruling house or zodiac, we all feel the effects much more intensely.

## Zodiacs

Similar to the houses, whichever zodiac sign a planet retrogrades in is going to make a difference in how that retrograde is felt. Let's take Mercury retrogrades in 2022 as an example. They all started in the early side of air signs, and they all ended in the later end of earth signs. In 2023, they begin in late earth signs and then retrograde back into earth signs. And in 2024, they'll begin in earth signs and retrograde back into fire signs.

"Each year brings its own special Mercury retrograde qualities," Wilkinson says. "Because each one falls in a different sign and in a different house, we're continually reviewing and getting new information and taking a new look at those affairs—just from a different angle."

So, say Mercury retrograde began in Aquarius. That's a visionary, idealistic sign. And then say it ended in Capricorn, which is a very practical sign. We can use that retrograde period to explore the practicality of our wildest dreams. Or, perhaps Mercury retrograde began in Gemini, which is all about information and sending and receiving ideas. And then the retrograde period ends in Taurus, which challenges us to simplify things and put some value into those ideas. With that transit, we should be thinking about how to add value to the information we received from the start, so that it can become a substantial idea by the end of the transit.

For each retrograde period, you'll need to take into consideration the sign each planet is retrograding into, and what that might mean for you specifically. Use the following list as a quick guide, noting that the date ranges are for each zodiac sign (your sun sign) and don't correspond to the zodiac signs that rule the houses. More information can be found on page 40 and in Chapter 14.

**Aries (March 21 to April 19).** Fire sign. Aries represents spontaneity, courage, competition, bravery, urgency, and decisiveness. Ruling planet: Mars.

**Taurus (April 20 to May 20).** Earth sign. Taurus represents reservation, resilience, persistence, patience, commitment, calmness, sensuality, stability, possession, and material wealth. Ruling planet: Venus.

**Gemini (May 21 to June 20).** Air sign. Gemini represents playfulness, variety, stimulation, duality, learning, communication, adaptability, social interaction, and curiosity. Ruling planet: Mercury.

**Cancer (June 21 to July 22).** Water sign. Cancer represents vulnerability, protection, intuition, emotion, caregiving, cultivation, motherhood, familiarity, security, tenacity, instinct, and empathy. Ruling planet: moon.

**Leo (July 23 to August 22).** Fire sign. Leo represents charisma, fun, dignity, confidence, generosity, motivation, creativity, inspiration, support, strength, courage, pride, authority, showmanship, integrity, accomplishment, and optimism. Ruling planet: sun.

**Virgo (August 23 to September 22).** Earth sign. Virgo represents efficiency, order, craft, communication, teamwork, development, practicality, health, perfectionism, organization, and humility. Ruling planet: Mercury.

**Libra (September 23 to October 22).** Air sign. Libra represents symmetry, balance, diplomacy, grace, civility, harmony, consideration, justice, objectivity, indecision, relationships, art, and compromise. Ruling planet: Venus.

**Scorpio (October 23 to November 21).** Water sign. Scorpio represents transformation, willpower, strength, resilience, passion, courage, survival, self-control, intuition, loyalty, jealousy, and domination. Ruling planets: Mars and Pluto.

**Sagittarius (November 22 to December 21).** Fire sign. Sagittarius represents optimism, travel, movement, social interaction, exploration, discovery, adventure, meaning, confidence, freedom, possibility, philosophy, education, religion, opportunity, and honesty. Ruling planet: Jupiter.

**Capricorn (December 22 to January 19).** Earth sign. Capricorn represents focus, strategy, achievement, patience, endurance, introversion, tradition, structure, self-reliance, ambition, reliability, and purpose. Ruling planet: Saturn.

**Aquarius (January 20 to February 18).** Air sign. Aquarius represents independence, awareness, determination, individuality, enlightenment, knowledge, community, change, creativity, and rationality. Ruling planets: Saturn and Uranus.

**Pisces (February 19 to March 20).** Water sign. Pisces represents emotion, freedom, sacrifice, art, imagination, sensitivity, retreat, compassion, devotion, romance, and selflessness. Ruling planets: Jupiter and Neptune.

You may have noticed that each zodiac sign has its own ruling planet. If a planet retrogrades in its own sign, the effects of that transit can be a bit more chaotic or intense.

# Distance

The distance between a planet and the sun can alter how intense the retrograde effects are and how they impact individuals and the world. The further out a planet is, the less likely we are to feel its impact. We'll still get it, for sure, but we may not notice it outright. It could be something working in the background, or something affecting everyone on a global level rather than a personal one.

The planets can be broken down into three categories depending on how far they are from the sun.

- Mercury, Venus, and Mars are considered personal planets, and so are the sun and moon. They're all located on the Earth side of the asteroid belt between Mars and Jupiter. They affect us directly—our instincts, how we communicate, how we relate to others, and how assertive we are.

- Jupiter and Saturn are considered social planets, which means they represent us within the context of our relationships with family and society as a whole. They're at the middle of the planetary spread. These two planets govern things like faith, boundaries, expanding our minds, and bringing outward influences inward.

- The final grouping—Uranus, Neptune, and Pluto—are the collective planets. They're the furthest out and have the slowest orbits. They represent entire eras and what the political and social ideals are at the time. So things like enlightenment, transformation, and devotion.

When the planets go retrograde, they tend to have an effect based on what they're classified as, in addition to how strong the impact is. So the furthest out planets will, perhaps, change how the world as a whole (and us as part of a group) handles transformations. And the closest planets will affect something directly in our sphere of influence, like when communication goes haywire during Mercury retrograde.

## Updated Star Charts

Every few years, a (false) rumor pops up that NASA introduced a new zodiac sign: Ophiuchus. The dates for this thirteenth zodiac sign are November 29 to December 17. Taking this new sign into consideration, all the other signs would have to shift to include it, which would mean your sign might be different from what you thought. And since retrogrades in your sun sign can feel a little different to you than they do to everyone else, you may have to rethink your whole strategy of managing them. (A sun sign determines your zodiac sign at birth, referring to the position of the sun when you were born and which zodiac constellation was hidden behind it.)

With Ophiuchus included, these are the dates for the updated zodiac. You'll notice the date ranges here overlap. That's because with Ophiuchus added, the time of day you were born would cause your sign to shift as well—so someone born in the morning on February 16 might have a different sign than someone born in the evening on February 16.

- **Capricorn:** January 20 to February 16

- **Aquarius:** February 16 to March 11

- **Pisces:** March 11 to April 18

- **Aries:** April 18 to May 13

- **Taurus:** May 13 to June 21

- **Gemini:** June 21 to July 20

- **Cancer:** July 20 to August 10

- **Leo:** August 10 to September 16

- **Virgo:** September 16 to October 30

- **Libra:** October 30 to November 23

- **Scorpio:** November 23 to November 29

- **Ophiuchus:** November 29 to December 17

- **Sagittarius:** December 17 to January 20

As a stereotypical Leo (who is a Leo even with this update), I can confidently say, *Back off, November. Why should you get all the extra attention?*

In actuality, though, your sun sign hasn't changed. And even NASA confirms it.[3] The extra sign was already around when ancient Babylonians mapped the constellations. They just decided to leave it out. We don't know why. Maybe they just wanted nice, even math, so they went with 12 signs instead.

"As an astrologer, I can assure you that your zodiac sign didn't change," author and astrologer Nina Kahn tells Reuters. "Ophiuchus is a real constellation, but it's not a zodiac sign. As you may know, there are many constellations in the sky, but not all of them are included in the zodiac."[4] The sky has 88 official constellations, per the International Astronomical Union. The zodiac only includes the 12 the sun passes through as we view them from Earth.

---

3  "Constellations and the Calendar," NASA.tumblr.com, July 17, 2012, https://nasa.tumblr.com /post/150688852794/zodiac.

4  Reuters Fact Check, "Fact Check-False Posts about NASA Changing the Zodiac Resurface," May 28, 2021, https://www.reuters.com/article/factcheck-nasa-zodiac/fact-check-false-posts -about-nasa-changing-the-zodiac-resurface-idUSL2N2NF2AW.

So, to finally put to rest this recurring rumor of a new zodiac sign—yours didn't change. And no, there's no effect on retrogrades in your sign.

# Degree Theory

If you've taken a close look at your birth chart (What are you waiting for if you haven't? Go! Go!), you've probably noticed either the set of numbers next to each planet or the tick marks all the way around the circle of the chart. These are the degrees of your chart.

Like all perfect circles, your birth chart is 360 degrees around. Each zodiac sign occupies 30 degrees, beginning at zero and ending at 29, when the next zodiac sign begins. The numbers next to each planet on your chart indicate at what degree of the zodiac that planet falls. For even more detail, you may also see a number right after the degree. That's the minute marking. Some planets fall between degrees, and the minute marking lets you know what point of that 60-second span of the zodiac they're at. So, if Mercury is at 16 degrees and 42 seconds in Virgo in your chart, it'll look like this next to the planet: 16°42'.

If you have a more simplified chart, the degrees may be grouped into decans, or sets of ten degrees each. The first decan covers degrees 0 to 9; the second decan covers degrees 10 to 19; and the third decan covers degrees 20 to 29. With this type of chart, you'll have to guess at the exact degree each planet falls. You can get extra fancy and use a protractor if you want. Or…just get another chart that has all the degrees on it.

Some astrologers use a system called degree theory, which places more layers of meaning on the planets in your chart depending on their degree. In this system, if a planet falls closer to the degree extremes (0 or 29), it doesn't interact as strongly with the zodiac sign it's in—or the zodiac has a delayed influence on the planet. The closer that planet gets to the middle of the zodiac degree, with 15 being the zenith, the stronger its influence will be over your life and the deeper interaction it'll have with that zodiac sign. (Fifteen is the middle of the degrees for each zodiac and represents the main issues in that sign. More on this in Critical Degrees below.)

So let's say you have Venus in Leo at 15 degrees. (Remember, this doesn't mean Leo is your sun sign. This is only about Venus's placement in the sky when you were born.) Venus is the planet of love, and Leo is known for confidence. Because Venus is at the middle (15) of the degree span, you would feel the full interaction between the two planets in your life, so you may be quite confident in relationships, or even overconfident. If Venus were in Leo at something closer to 29 degrees, you might lack confidence in relationships or begin to gain that confidence as the relationship lasts longer and longer.

Degree theory is the reason it's so important to have all the information correct on your birth chart (i.e., location, day, and time). A matter of seconds can change your chart completely.

"I have an astrologer, Ray," Salomon says. "He's like a million years old and he was looking at my chart and we were having a conversation about it. He's like, I don't think you were born at 12:25. I think it was 12:26 based on [your personality]. I was like, that makes more sense. It changes the degree up just enough to make some sort of change."

## Critical Degrees

In degree theory, some degrees are more important than others—or at least more strongly felt. These are called critical degrees, and they bring both the best and the worst of each zodiac sign. You'll have deeper challenges if one of your planets hits one of these degrees, but you'll also have better insight into how you can make that aspect of the zodiac work best for you and your future.

"If you have a critical degree in your chart, you are more likely to face challenges in that sign until the time comes that you transmute that challenge into your greatest strength," astrologer Emily Ridout says.

"Once transmuted, critical degrees carry a weight of great power and influence."[5]

In general, the critical degrees are 0, 15, and 29.

Zero is the ingress, and it marks the second a planet enters a new sign. It's the very beginning of that astrological season, when everything is fresh and new.

As mentioned, fifteen is the middle of the degrees for each zodiac. It represents the main issues in that sign. If you have a planet at 15 in a fixed sign, it's called the avatar degree and means that everyone you know comes to you for help, reassurance, care, or really anything they might need. You're the dependable and reliable go-to person.

Twenty-nine is the anaretic degree. This is the last spot a planet hits before moving into another sign. It represents completion on a karmic level, when you have everything you need to master your own zodiac sign—and you likely have an overall higher purpose or are often considered an old soul.

Each zodiac sign has its own set of critical degrees, too, based on the sign's mode, which is either cardinal (the signs that begin each season), fixed (the signs that begin in the middle of each season), or mutable (the signs that begin at the end of each season). Here's what they are:

| Sign Type | Signs | Degrees |
| --- | --- | --- |
| CARDINAL | Aries, Cancer, Libra, Capricorn | 0, 13, 26 |
| FIXED | Taurus, Leo, Scorpio, Aquarius | 8, 9, 21, and 22 |
| MUTABLE | Gemini, Virgo, Sagittarius, Pisces | 4 and 17 |

## Cusps

I hate to tell you all, especially you astrological sign wafflers, but cusps aren't real. The degrees around the zodiac are so precise that being

---

5  Astrology.com, "What Is Degree Theory?," accessed July 28, 2023, https://www.astrology.com/article/degree-theory-astrology.

on the "cusp" of two signs isn't going to make any bit of difference. If your sun is at 29 degrees in Aquarius, you're just as much an Aquarius as someone with their sun in 3 degrees. That being said, your exact birth time can affect your sun sign—so two people born on February 19 could be respectively an Aquarius at 29 degrees or a Pisces at zero degrees.

So how do all of these degrees affect retrogrades? Well, you can imagine that if one of your planetary degrees is super intense in one of the zodiac signs, that might change how intensely you feel it when that planet retrogrades. Using the example from above, if you have Venus at 15 degrees Leo, your confidence in your relationship might *really* falter during a Venus retrograde in Leo. If your Venus is closer to 29 degrees Leo, that same retrograde will probably be less intense.

# Dispositor

A dispositor is a planet that rules over a sign that another planet may be stationed in. For example, Mars rules Aries. When another planet, like Jupiter, is in Aries, Mars is the dispositor of Jupiter. That means Jupiter is going to behave like Mars while Jupiter is in Aries, and will have Martian influences when it retrogrades.

There's also something in astrology called the final dispositor. This is a single planet that rules over your entire chart. To find it, you have to make a kind of flow chart that narrows your birth chart down to a single planet based on which planets are dispositing which. In some cases, you won't have a final dispositor, for example, if no planet is in its own sign, or if multiple planets are in their own sign. It sounds confusing, so here's an example using my own birth chart.

| Symbols of the Planets and Signs | | | |
|---|---|---|---|
| ☉ = Sun | ♄ = Saturn | ♈ = Aries | ♎ = Libra |
| ☽ = Moon | ♅ = Uranus | ♉ = Taurs | ♏ = Scorpio |
| ☿ = Mercury | ♆ = Neptune | ♊ = Geminio | ♐ = Sagittarius |
| ♀ = Venus | ♇ = Pluto | ♋ = Cancer | ♑ = Capricorn |
| ♂ = Mars | ☊ = N. Node | ♌ = Leo | ♒ = Aquarius |
| ♃ = Jupiter | R = Retrograde | ♍ = Virgo | ♓ = Pisces |

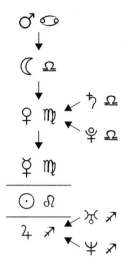

My chart does not have a final dispositor. Mars is in Cancer, which is ruled by the moon. The moon is Libra, which is ruled by Venus. Venus is in Virgo, which is ruled by Mercury. Mercury is in Virgo, which is its ruling planet. I also have the sun in Leo, which it rules, and Jupiter in Sagittarius, which it rules.

When a planet retrogrades in its ruling sign, we feel the effects acutely—especially if it's your ruling planet, and even more so if it's your final dispositor! Everything will seem more intense.

## Joint Retrogrades

Having one planet retrograde is really common, and for astrologers, it's pretty much business as usual when up to three planets retrograde at the same time. Four planets retrograding at once doesn't happen too often, and five at once is just plain rare, happening only about 4 percent of the time each century. Even still, in 2022, six planets were retrograde at the same time.

It's a complicated transit for us when different planets retrograde together. Instead of managing just one retrograde's effect, we have to factor in the effects of several other planets. And it's not always a great thing. Some planetary retrogrades, when you put their energies together, can be pretty destructive.

Take Saturn and Mars, for example. Saturn rules discipline and structure. Mars is a fiery energy that encourages us to take charge and initiate things. But if the two retrograde together, that could cause a lot of chaos thanks to the opposing energies.

It could be that you lose a job or majorly mess up a project, or you may even just fly off the handle a little, because Saturn's retrograde brings in a lack of discipline and self-control, paired with the volatile Mars energy.

"It just gives me a bad feeling," Salomon says of that particular joint retrograde.

Venus and Jupiter retrograding together are another cause for a bit of concern. They're both signs of luck and expansion, so when they have a joint retrograde, we should be prepared to lose a lot of money or have massively bad luck. Saturn and Pluto retrograding together can create a ton of problems on the world scale, and it takes us a while to deal with the reverberations from that. The two planets are conjunct in 40-year cycles, so the effects last for a long time.

At this point, you may be wondering if all eight planets (Mercury, Venus, Mars, Jupiter, Saturn, Uranus, Neptune, and Pluto) can retrograde at the same time? It seems like the entire world would melt down if something like that were to happen.

Sadly, I can't reassure you that such a phenomenon hasn't and will never happen in the history and future of the cosmos. But it would be exceedingly rare if it did—to the tune of seven times in 30,000 years, according to an anonymous mathematician who calculated out the possibility online using an ephemeris, which is a book of charts showing all the positions of all the planets (including the sun and moon) in future years.[6] Extrapolating that out, we wouldn't see this happen for more than 15,000 years from now. Humanity would probably be extinct by that point, or at least living on a different planet or spot in the universe, which would render our earthly retrogrades irrelevant. So, basically, don't worry about it.

Of course, it's also possible for none of the planets to be retrograde at all—when they're all direct in the sky.

"Think of harmonics and symphony and music to understand the planetary motions," Mihas says. "When all the planets are direct, it's kind of like the cosmic symphony is well-tuned and harmonized."

If you look at your birth chart and see nary a retrograde in it, that's great news for you. Mihas shares the story of a woman; let's call her Stephanie. Stephanie had no retrogrades at all in her birth chart. All her planets were fast and direct. She was a New Yorker; she grew up in New York and stayed in the city as she got older. But one day, she decided she wanted to leave New York and go to train horses for her career. Within six months, she was already well on her way to doing just that. She was working with horses in Central Park and, just like the planets in her chart, had moved quickly and directly into the life she wanted to have, even though she still lived in New York at the time. Without any retrogrades in her chart, she didn't have the typical blockages that most of us would have. It helped her move forward in her life a lot easier.

6    "Can Eight Retrograde (Seen from Earth) Planets Occur?," Astronomy StackExchange, last accessed July 6, 2023, https://astronomy.stackexchange.com/questions/32426/can-eight -retrograde-seen-from-earth-planets-occur.

# SECTION II

## PLANET-BY-PLANET RETROGRADE GUIDE

# Chapter 5

# MERCURY

WARNING! WARNING! MERCURY IS IN RETROGRADE!

…Maybe.

You may say it is, your friends may say it is, some rando on the street may say it is…but do you really know for sure? (The answer will be "yes," once you've finished this book.)

Mercury retrograde is a buzz phrase, something people use to explain away everything bad that happens to them throughout the year. It makes sense, of course. Mercury retrogrades more than any other planet. So at least half the time, you and your friends and that rando are probably right. It retrogrades so often because it's the fastest planet—so you can expect it to retrograde two or more times per year. And we notice its retrograde a lot more than the other planets', particularly the outer planets. They're so slow that they're retrograde about half the year anyway. Mercury retrograde practically brings a parade to announce itself.

"Mercury being so fast, it's a much more jarring, recognizable energy," Kurtz says. "The other planets are so slow that it's a very slow crescendo for their energy. It shifts very slowly and it's almost like you've been hearing this buzzing sound in the background, very quietly at first and then louder. But because it's been growing in volume so quietly, your brain just tunes it out. With Mercury, it's much more like, 'Well, I'm here.'"

The planet orbits so quickly because it's the closest to the sun. It takes only 88 days for Mercury to do a full trip around our central star. And because it's retrograde so regularly and because the planet rules communication, we've got more opportunities to notice it. Not just because everyone talks about it (hey, communication!), but because Mercury also represents our thinking mind, our divine mind—something we're conscious of every second of every day.

Our minds really never stop. They're always racing forward, thinking ever more into the future. And then eventually, they have to slow down so life can actually catch up with us. And when they do, we usually enter a period of introspection. We look inward; we look backward. We review and reflect until we've looked at an aspect of our lives long enough to move forward. And then we do, starting the cycle all over again.

"Mercury is how we coordinate things in life, so sometimes our minds get out ahead of our lives, and we have to slow down and figure out how all of this information fits into our lives on a day-to-day basis," Wilkinson says.

Mercury almost gives us a *Back-to-the-Future*-type feeling. If there's something we didn't deal with in the past or something we let go of, it's going to pop back up right now to say hello. Mercury might bring back to the forefront something you dealt with very publicly, or something that was subconscious or concealed. And since you would've gone through some time with Mercury direct between what happened and the current retrograde period, you're able to take a new look at the past, a look that's informed by new knowledge.

Whatever that thing is could even be something you thought just wasn't all that important anymore. But once Mercury retrograde comes around and brings it back up, you'll see it in a new light, with a new understanding. You might realize that thing, the one that's no longer important, was actually crucial to how you're functioning now.

Think of it like flipping a coin to see where you should move next. (Hey, don't knock it; that's partially how I met my husband!) You flip the coin, you make the move, and you begin to live your life. You forget about how you flipped that coin, because it's no longer important. But when Mercury retrograde starts drudging all those feelings and emotions up again, you can look around at what you've accomplished (like gaining a wife, perhaps), and realize that coin flip was more important that you thought.

And truly, that's exactly what a retrograde—any retrograde, not just Mercury's—does. It brings back echoes of the past, reviews and reflections for us to deal with so we can move forward. And sometimes, the retrograde is more a rehearsal than anything else.

"Sometimes during a retrograde, we go through something and it doesn't turn out the way we thought, and we wonder why we went through it," Wilkinson says. "Then we find ourselves doing the exact same thing a year later, *when* we're supposed to be doing it, *the way* we're supposed to be doing it."

Only at that point can we sit and really enjoy and embrace the retrograde period we're going through. Now we've got the expertise necessary to manage it well and learn from it.

Astrologers seem to be split on whether or not Mercury retrograde is a difficult one or something we should treasure. King, for one, puts it in the difficult camp.

"My least favorite is Mercury retrograde due to its frequency and its tendency to create misfired conversations between two or more people," she says. "Given that life is lived in the company of others, this can be quite pesky and frustrating."

Atlas, though, sees it as something special.

"As someone with several retrograde planets, I personally enjoy the brief downtime that Mercury retrograde offers," she says. "While it's not the easiest as far as communications go, it's a wonderful time to pull back from the hamster wheel, lock yourself in your writing cave, and tackle the to-do list you've been putting off for a long time. As someone who enjoys revisiting old writings and ideas, this cycle supports going back and making the most of these things."

Oliver is a little different and sees the duality of Mercury's retrograde period. It's both good *and* tough.

"I would say Mercury retrogrades are the most challenging, mostly because they show up the most often," Oliver says. "So, we're dealing with three Mercury retrogrades at the minimum every year. [But] I actually really like Mercury retrogrades. I was born with natal Mercury retrograde in Virgo as it was stationing direct, and I think that it's a really good time for reevaluating and redoing things that you couldn't really get done the first time; you couldn't really figure out exactly how they were supposed to go. It gives you a little bit of a reset."

Javor agrees.

"I actually don't mind Mercury retrograde as long as I have the time and space to be able to slow down and unplug a little bit," she says. "I find that when I can do that, when I can take some days off-line, maybe just to wander around my neighborhood and write in my journal, then it's actually quite lovely."

She likens it to the writing process. At some point after you've written something, you'll need to go back over everything to edit it, fact-check it, redo anything that needs to be spruced up. If you're doing that, the writing process doesn't have to be a challenge. And if you treat Mercury retrograde the same way—reflecting over what's happened, making changes as needed—it doesn't have to be challenging either. It only becomes harder when you resist the natural flow of energy that Mercury sends out.

There are essentially two uses for the period. One is practical in the astrological sense; the other is spiritual. On the practical end, Mercury retrograde can bring awareness to situations, so you might take the time to ask yourself some questions, like "Would it help for me to send an email to myself before I send it to other people?" or "Was it *really* Mercury retrograde that made me send a text to my ex/that canceled my flight/that made me fight with my neighbor?" Reflecting on the retrograde can help you a bit with your future decision-making in these situations, as long as you remember that during Mercury's transit backward, sometimes squirrely stuff just happens.

On a spiritual level, really investigating the things going on during Mercury retrograde can show you there's an underlying order to everything. It can almost validate your own life experiences—and that's something that can be immensely useful for the future.

Mercury is also the perfect example of what people get wrong about retrogrades. There's so much fear because everyone around us who's even mildly into astrological things hypes it up so much. Mercury on the whole is a pretty mild retrograde compared to some of the others. But you might never have known that because people act like it's the end of the world.

"Most of the time, when someone says their life is in shambles because of Mercury retrograde, you can bet they're probably having another challenging personal transit from Saturn or Pluto that is the culprit for their woes more than the retrograde itself," Atlas says. "The other thing most people misunderstand is that each planetary retrograde has its own themes. You're not likely to experience miscommunications or tech issues with Mars or Venus retrograde because those are Mercury retrograde issues. Getting to know the nuances of the planets and their specific energy will help you prepare for each of the retrogrades."

That being said, though, it might be a good thing for astrology overall that everyone gets all worked up about Mercury all the time. Mercury retrograde definitely has a reputation for being absolutely awful for everyone, but that's partly because the public conversation around astrology has been incredibly simplified. When you look deeper into it, you find that astrology is quite complicated (the subject of entire books, even!) and can't necessarily be distilled into something like a single article about how you probably shouldn't send out that nasty email to your boss when Mercury's retrograde (or let's be real, at any time).

"Part of me is like, Oh, all the jokes about Mercury retrograde and Mercury in Gatorade and all those memes and stuff, I think they're hilarious," Norton says. "And part of me is like, Oh, it's getting overblown now, nobody really understands what it is. But another part of me sees they're talking about astrology, and that's great. So, it's kind of like there's no bad press because all of that is about astrology and making astrology more important, and it's becoming a hugely popular area for people."

She hopes that the heightened discourse around retrogrades will encourage people to find a real astrologer who can give them detailed information about their charts and personal astrology—because that could really help their lives.

"Astrology can go both ways," she says. "It can be completely meaningless and trite, or it can actually really help you manage your life. So, it's all good that we're all talking about it. It leads to curiosity."

# Mercury Retrograde in History

Mercury retrograde has had its astrological hand in a huge number of meaningful events throughout history. According to Wilkinson, Mercury retrograde coincides with moments of uncovering past corporate criminal activity, exposing wrongdoing (and wrongdoers), bringing the hidden to light, seeing the past creep back up, and enduring major turning points and developments. Here's a brief sampling, compiled by Wilkinson, of such moments:

- When Columbus set sail in 1492 to the Americas, he didn't know where he was headed. He also didn't know where he was when he finally got there, and he wasn't completely sure where he'd come from when he got back to Spain. That's a travel blunder if there's ever been one.

- The Spanish Armada set sail to invade England. Unexpected storms in the North Atlantic in 1588 destroyed the armada and ruined Spain's prowess as a global sea power. Imagine trying to travel for an invasion, and instead, your whole reputation collapses.

- In 1870, women in Utah gained the right to vote—well before women gained that same right on a national level. This event hits Mercury's communication, learning, and ideas traits. Earning this right took a lot of protesting and making intentions known— many people hadn't even considered letting women vote, so it was a new idea as well. And today, communication about this is still behind; knowledge of the event isn't widely spread.

- From April 14 to 15, 1912, the *Titanic* sank. Travel and communication! For one, the *Titanic* was a steamer *traveling* to New York. And secondly, communication broke down more than once before the events of that fateful day. One of the Marconi systems stopped working the day before the crash, and the men working the telegraph had to fix it. Then, for whatever reason, messages about heavy ice in the area didn't make it to the ship's captain. And once the boat was sinking, SOS transmissions received very few responses, even though some other vessels were nearby.

- The Russian army invaded Finland in 1939, starting the Winter War. It ended not even four months later in a massive loss for the Russians. The Russian army wasn't familiar with the landscape of Suomussalmi, where the war largely took place. So, even though they had a much higher number of soldiers than the Finns did, they didn't understand what to do. It's a classic example of making a big and rash decision during Mercury retrograde—and then facing the consequences.

- The Nazis spent a Mercury retrograde period during World War II confiscating French art treasures. A few years later, that artwork was recovered from a salt mine—also during Mercury retrograde.

- Mexico declared war against Germany, Italy, and Japan on May 30, 1942, and then agreed the war had been underway since May 22. Hello, lack of proper communication!

- Xerox and fax machines made their official debut in 1948, introducing the world to an all-new way to communicate.

- In 2000, the election between George W. Bush and Al Gore went to the Supreme Court over hanging chads—which was really a breakdown in communication between voters and the government thanks to faulty ballots.

- The 2020 election was the same day Mercury retrograde ended, and it was hallmarked by miscommunication and misinformation.

And that's just a tiny selection of all the things that have happened on a major world scale during Mercury retrograde. You may have noticed a lot of these events are connected to a breakdown in communication or travel.

# Communication and Mercury Retrograde

You may know Mercury as the Roman messenger god, a counterpoint to the Greek Hermes. Mythological depictions show him with wings on his shoes and helmet, often in motion, running quickly to deliver messages to the other gods or to communicate between the underworld and the living world. So, it only makes sense that Mercury the planet rules communication and that when it goes retrograde, we hear about it nonstop.

At that point, we really need to slow down. Expect delays. Expect misunderstandings. These are givens with Mercury retrograde. But if we don't take the time to acknowledge that and prepare for it, the retrograde period can really wreak havoc on your whole life.

That can manifest as arguments or poor choices, like emailing your ex, technology snafus, miscommunications, and writings that are riddled with mistakes. That being said, we can't blame Mercury for our problems when it's retrograde—even though we so often do.

"It's not so much that Mercury is making you bad at communication or is the cause of the fact that you missed your bus and you forgot to plug your phone in last night," Oliver says. "It's mindlessness that really comes to the surface there. The opportunity for accidents is heightened. Being bad at communication is definitely a thing, like we kind of got our wires crossed during Mercury retrograde. But if you're just ghosting somebody, that's a you problem, not a Mercury problem."

Since we use our technological devices to communicate, you can be sure there's going to be some technological issues during Mercury retrograde as well. We're connected all the time, to every bit of tech around us, asking it questions ("Hey Alexa, what's the weather?") or telling it what to do ("Siri, play music for a road trip."), and we relied on it even more during the recent COVID-19 pandemic. Astrologically, we're relying on Mercury to keep all these fancy communication devices working properly.

"We are really Mercury's bitch in this world," Norton says. "It's a very basic component of human behavior to give and receive messages. So, when that's kind of wonky, then you can expect it to affect everything."

Maybe power at the local radio station goes out, or you lose your Wi-Fi for a few days. Try to laugh about it, and then use that experience as a push to have a better setup by the time the next Mercury retrograde rolls around.

# Traveling with Mercury Retrograde

In the last week of 2022, Southwest Airlines had a meltdown. There was a massive winter storm in late December, which led to airlines canceling a large number of flights. Typical for a big storm, right? Well, while other airlines regained their footing, Southwest continued to trip and fall. More and more flights were canceled. Families were stranded at the airport over Christmas, and people were huddled on floors to sleep. Luggage went pretty much everywhere except the airport it needed to be at, leaving people without vital medications, spare clothes, or the basic necessities to make being stuck at an airport the tiniest bit more manageable. Customer service agents weren't incredibly helpful, either, if you could get through to one. Travelers spent hours on hold just to get nowhere, both literally and metaphorically.

For days after all other airlines were back on schedule, Southwest continued to cancel flights. They blamed it on the weather, but after a while, the truth came out: all those cancelations were thanks in part to outdated internal software.

Most airlines use what's called a *hub-and-spoke* system, which means flights are routed through larger airports. It means a layover for you and cost savings for the airline. But Southwest uses a *point-to-point* system, where flights don't head through a central hub—they go directly to the final destination. It takes less time for flights and is usually less of a hassle for the traveler, but it's incredibly complicated to manage scheduling for planes, passengers, pilots, and crew, especially when an airline that is using severely outdated computer software to do so, like Southwest was. Flight attendants and pilots had been telling the airline that systems needed to be updated for years, but nothing had changed.

"We're still using not only IT from the '90s, but also processes [from] when our airline was a tenth of the size," the president of the union representing Southwest pilots told NPR at the time. "And it's really just not scaled for an operation that we have today."[7]

All told, by the time the whole debacle had ended, Southwest had canceled more than 16,700 flights. It cost the airline about $800 million when you factor in refunds, reimbursement for rebooked flights on other airlines, returned loyalty points, and handouts of extra frequent flyer points. The US Department of Transportation even launched an investigation into the airline, noting that it potentially created impossible flight schedules in the lead-up to the disaster.

Here's something you probably won't find very shocking at all: Mercury was retrograde when all this went down. Mercury governs all modes of transportation—planes, trains, cars, boats—anything that can take you on a short journey. So when the planet retrogrades, it can cause a lot of travel challenges.

The Southwest debacle was a classic and right-on-the-money example of Mercury retrograde. Any decent astrologer knows to expect delays in travel when the planet runs backward in the sky. And now, you know too!

"It was a shitshow," Mihas says, noting that when Mercury was station, appearing stopped in the sky, that's when the whole situation was at its worst.

Astrologers have a ton of advice for ensuring travel during Mercury retrograde goes off without a hitch. Mihas suggests taking actions as simple as getting to the airport a little bit earlier than you normally would. Of course, getting there early doesn't mean you won't have to deal with any flight drama—but it gives you more time to do so.

---

7   Camila Domonoske, "5 Things to Know about Southwest's Disastrous Meltdown," NPR, December 30, 2022, https://www.npr.org/2022/12/30/1146377342/5-things-to-know -about-southwests-disastrous-meltdown.

"Even if I get to the airport earlier, that doesn't mean the flight won't get canceled," she says. "But, you know, if I am able to put in a little bit more effort that may be [helpful]. I mean, I had a Mercury retrograde where it was about two hours of traffic on the way to the airport. So, I was happy I went a little earlier."

Levitt's suggestion is even more intense: Give yourself an entire extra day to travel. She uses traveling to a wedding in wine country as an example.

"A lot of people come up to the wine country and they have weddings there. If it's Mercury retrograde, that's not so much bad for a wedding, but don't have them fly in that Saturday morning and then drive out to Napa or Sonoma. Come in that Friday afternoon, spend the night if possible, and be prepared for the next day. Plan the extra day for guests. [If you don't], the catering might go to the wrong place or flowers aren't correct, and everyone is still trying to arrive that day."

Weddings aside, you ultimately just want to give yourself enough time to handle things in case something goes wrong. And be prepared for that, as well. Triple-check for your passport and your tickets. Pay extra attention to the terminal and gate you need to head to, so you don't accidentally end up at the international terminal for a domestic flight. Book yourself a longer layover than you normally would so you have enough time to transit to your next flight.

"Here's an example," Levitt says. "You're always chaotic at the airport. Well, don't live like that anymore. Clearly, it's not going to work in the long run or even now in the short run. Don't do that."

Be sure you're paying extra attention and getting all your ducks in a row before you fly, drive, take the train, board a cruise, walk somewhere, or just generally travel. Awareness of the retrograde cycle and knowing how to meet it head-on is the perk of astrology every time Mercury goes retrograde. You've probably learned from past travel experiences and can put that knowledge into action now.

Other travel tips for Mercury retrograde? Don't fly if it's around Christmastime (when Mercury is almost always retrograde). Instead, choose an alternate mode of transportation or just stay home. Travel on a Tuesday or Thursday if you must travel. And if you absolutely have to go somewhere, visit a place you've been before. That way, you know the way there and you know what to expect as soon as you arrive.

## Tips for Managing Mercury

Since this retrograde period is the one we deal with most often *and* the one we get the most worried about, how about some tips from astrologers to ensure you're using the transit to your best advantage? Here's what a few had to say about it:

LEVITT: Do exactly what Mercury when it's going backward would imply: retrograde. Review, redo, reassess. Catch up on what you've been doing for the last four months or quarter of the year. So, stop and organize or pay your taxes or follow up or clean your computer, anything Mercurial in nature. And then move forward after the three weeks are over. And since Mercury is retrograde, allow more time [for things to go wrong]. Like for surgery, check if it's a different location than where you usually see your doctor, and look for paperwork problems like billing for insurance.

KURTZ: It's really just a reminder to slow down, that it's the time to say, "Okay, I need to not completely overbook myself. I need to not make any immediate rash decisions. This is the time that I can really sit and think about what I want to do, how I'm doing things, what is going on." It's like a mental check-in that we get every year, two to three times a year, and people tend to feel rushed through it. But that's not what it's about. It's a time to slow down and really think about why you feel like you need to take on 12 million projects at once. Why do you feel like you need to make that major decision right now, to sign that contract, to do that business move? Is that something that's actually in your best interest, or is that something that you feel like you need to do, but there isn't really a tangible reason behind it? Don't let the excessive Mercury energy take you off your feet.

NORTON: In our Western culture, we don't understand how to work with retrogrades. We're constantly moving forward, going, going, going, and it's the rat race that we're all in. So when a retrograde happens, which is actually a gift to us, we look the gift horse right in the mouth and just try to move forward. And because our lives are ruled by technology and Mercury rules technology, that's the primary way that we all get a little bit twisted. Take some time instead to explore the gift.

# Ritual for Mercury Retrograde

*Dear Mercury: Please stop making communication a nightmare. Love, everyone on planet Earth.*

Do you think it listened to us? Probably not. Mercury's connection with communication and technology can make pretty much every attempt at conversation a disaster. So, for this ritual, we're going to take something confusing and turn it into something that makes sense. If you've ever played the game Wordle this ritual will look familiar to you.

# CONFUSION TO CLARITY

**YOU'LL NEED:**

Two pieces of selenite, a crystal that enhances clarity and relieves anxiety

Two white candles, preferably unscented tealights

Two sets of alphabet cards (Note: You can easily buy these online or make your own by writing each letter of the alphabet on its own card.)

**DIRECTIONS:**

1.  Place the two pieces of selenite at arm's length in front of you. Since Mercury retrograde leads to communication mix-ups and heightened anxiety as a result, this crystal will both help and soothe you.

2.  Put one white candle to your left and one white candle to your right.

3.  Take from the alphabet cards the letters to spell CLEAR, LUCID, and POWER, or three words of your choice that convey clarity and precision. You can create more cards for specific letters if you need them.

4.  Shuffle all the cards together and lay them out in three lines in front of you. The point here is to misspell the words.

5.  Move the cards around to properly spell the first word. When you've finished, close your eyes and say, "My communication will be clear during Mercury retrograde."

6.  Move the cards around to properly spell the second word. When you've finished, close your eyes and say, "I will be a lucid thinker during Mercury retrograde."

7.  Move the cards around to properly spell the third word. When you've finished, close your eyes and say, "I have the power of clarity during Mercury retrograde."

8.  Meditate on your three words until you feel ready to move on with your day.

# Retrograde Review: Mercury

- **Frequency of retrograde:** 3 to 4 times a year

- **Retrograde tendencies:**

  » *Positive:* Allows us to get organized, explore past mistakes with communication and learn from them, and examine the state of our technological devices

  » *Negative:* Messes up travel, causes problems with communication, breaks technology

- Be prepared for things to go wrong during Mercury retrograde. You may have miscommunications, delays, and technology problems. Give yourself enough time to deal with these things and learn from any mistakes you made, like always getting to the airport with too little time to spare or relying too much on a digital day planner.

# Chapter 6

# VENUS

In ancient Mesopotamia, there was a goddess named Inanna (the Queen of Heaven). She governed love, fertility, and beauty. Her older sister, Ereshkigal, ruled the underworld. When Ereshkigal's husband died, Inanna descended into the underworld to attend the funeral rites. Ereshkigal was none too pleased about that, though, and forced Inanna to strip down on her way through the underworld's gates. Eventually, Inanna ended up as a corpse hanging on a wall to rot—not exactly the most sisterly behavior, if you ask me.

Inanna is revived a few days later, thanks to the efforts of her servant Ninshubur. But as with all mythological tales, Inanna couldn't just go on her merry way. Because she was officially a corpse in the underworld, her spot had to be filled by someone else when she left. When she returned to Heaven, she saw her husband, Dumuzid, happily sitting on his throne instead of mourning her. Enraged, she sent him to take her place. Dumuzid's sister, though, wasn't having it and volunteered to go in his place. The gods examined the situation and decided that Dumuzid would be in the underworld half the year, and his sister would be there the other half. That rising and descending resulted in the seasons we have today.

Inanna's descent is also symbolism for Venus retrograde. Her planet is Venus (goddess of love, right?), and before Venus retrogrades, we can see it on the western horizon. But during the retrograde, it disappears—like when Inanna goes into the underworld.

The Venus retrograde only happens once every year and a half, for about 42 days. The planet rules money, relationships, art, and pleasure.

# Vexes of Venus Retrograde

So, let's get the bad stuff out of the way first. When Venus goes retrograde, you can expect some fluctuations in your love life and money situation—and not always good fluctuations. From a 2 a.m. text from an old flame asking "u up?" to the personal realization of a bad spending habit (Do your crystals *really* need all those tiny chairs to sit in?), the shifts of Venus retrograde can be pretty emotional and sometimes a little bit judgy. (The answer is yes, Venus. They really do need all those little chairs.)

Mashi Salomon, owner of Light and Lavender, thinks Venus retrograde can possibly be one of the worst to go through. The planet's connection to relationships and indulgence can resurface any sexual trauma or intense relationship problems someone may have been through. If you're on a healing path, that can either help or hurt you. Either way, it's going to be emotional.

Astrologer KJ Atlas agrees that this retrograde period can be particularly difficult.

"Venus, being a personal planet that affects all the things that make life sweet, triggers trepidation when retrograde looms because there seems to be an air of fear around the loss of things important to us," she says.

Even if you know the Venus retrograde cycle inside and out, and know that removing distractions from your daily life can be useful during that period, it's still likely to feel uncomfortable. You'll still feel like garbage, at least a little bit, if you're going through relationship issues or having financial problems—both of which can easily happen during this particular retrograde period.

But it's not all bad news, thankfully.

## Insight and Clarity

Allemana says that if he had to choose a favorite retrograde, Venus would be the lucky winner.

"It's a retrograde that encourages solitude, connecting more deeply with your own inner values, and nurturing a relationship with yourself," he says. "It's a self-care transit. Venus direct is great, but that retrograde really brings that energy inward."

With this one, you'll want to take some time to evaluate yourself. Sit with a journal somewhere outside, in nature, and ask yourself important questions: How am I connecting to myself and taking care of myself? How am I connecting to the people important to me in my life? Where do our values meet and where do they conflict? Am I properly taking care of all my relationships and any romantic partners?

Once you have the answers to those questions—and any others that may arise in the course of your writing—you'll be able to spend a bit of time reflecting on what you're doing that's working, what isn't, and how you can improve your life and your relationships in these aspects.

"I would advise taking some time to yourself," Allemana says. "If you have the opportunity to spend some time in nature or do some meditation or spiritual ritual where you're connecting deeply inward, that would be ideal."

You may want to take the time when you get home to go through your budget and bank statements, as well, just to take stock of your spending habits and how those can also improve.

The main point here is to investigate your relationships, values, finances, and self-care methods and figure out how to be and do better. That being said, Venus retrograde and all this introspection can be tough for some people, particularly those who don't like to be alone or have trouble going inward and reevaluating their values. It can be an uncomfortable and frustrating addition to all the struggles they might be having already because of the retrograde.

And even if you love being alone and enjoy introspection, conflicts and relationship challenges can still pop up to say hello during Venus retrograde. It happens to everyone. No one is immune, especially because relationships, well, tend to involve more than one person. And that other person has their own free will to do whatever they want without thinking about how you're trying to handle Venus retrograde.

That could mean that someone you cared for in some way comes back into your life, and you start to feel the same way about them that you once did. And with Venus retrograde, it's likely it was a person or a feeling that you got lost in, that knocked you off your center. But that doesn't necessarily mean you need to do anything about it.

"Anytime something returns, it's not necessarily because we haven't dealt with it," Wilkinson says. "Sometimes we did deal with it and now we just get to take a look at it in our rearview mirror so that we can see that was then and this is now, and now I know why that had to come down the way it did."

You should also pay extra attention to when Venus and the sun are conjunct near the middle of Venus retrograde. At that time, there's usually some sort of insight or clarity about exactly what that specific retrograde period means for you. And if you're taking the time to meditate on the retrograde itself, that could be easy for you to discover.

# Ritual for Venus Retrograde

In this ritual, you'll be honing in on Venus retrograde's relationships focus. It's broken into three sections: the first for encouraging self-love, the second for boosting trust and confidence in coupledom, and the third for protecting yourself from messy exes who come wandering back this time of year.

# LETTERS FOR SELF-LOVE, CURRENT LOVE, AND PAST LOVE

**YOU'LL NEED:**

3 pieces of paper

1 black candle

1 black tourmaline

1 red candle

1 rose quartz

1 white candle

1 blue chalcedony

1 writing utensil of your choice

3 envelopes

Rose petals

A fireproof container

A lighter or matches

**DIRECTIONS:**

1. Lay your three pieces of paper in a row on a desk or a table with a chair. You'll be writing on these pages.

2. Above the paper on the left, put the black candle and black tourmaline. These symbolize your past relationships.

3. Above the paper in the middle, put the red candle and rose quartz. These symbolize your relationship with yourself.

4. Above the paper on the right, put the white candle and blue chalcedony. These symbolize your current or future relationship.

5. Light the candle on the left. On the paper, write a letter to someone you were in a past relationship with and don't have interest in anymore. Explain what you liked about them, why things didn't work out, and why it's better if you're apart. Let them know that you will not entertain ideas of rekindling the relationship.

6. Light the candle on the right. On the paper, write a letter to your current partner or to the partner you wish to have. Explain why you two are good together, list the positive aspects of your relationship, and state that you will stay together as long as it's right for you to do so.

7. Light the middle candle. On this paper, write a love letter to yourself. Write what you think is great about you and why. Explore every sense of yourself here, saying something positive about every aspect.

8. Fold the letters and place them into separate envelopes. Lay them on the table and scatter rose petals on top of them.

9. Take a deep breath, close your eyes, and repeat this incantation: "I am my beloved and my beloved is me. Guard my love in the form it should be." Picture energy flowing from you into the envelopes as you speak. With every repetition, imagine the envelopes glowing brighter. Finish repeating the incantation when you feel satisfied with the energy level.

10. Take all three envelopes outside and burn them in a fireproof container. Release the ashes into the wind.

## Retrograde Review: Venus

- **Frequency of retrograde:** Every 18 months

- **Retrograde tendencies:**

  » *Positive:* A self-care transit that allows you to work on your relationship with yourself, evaluate past relationships, and examine money issues to see what you can change

  » *Negative:* May prompt problems with love life and money or a resurgence of emotional trauma

- This retrograde transit will probably be uncomfortable in at least some way. Give yourself some grace. Sit alone out in nature and think about how you can better your relationships with yourself, others, and your finances. And definitely don't respond to the long-ago ex that reaches back out during this time!

# Chapter 7

# MARS

You probably wouldn't think of Mars—the planet representing destructive tendencies, war, and masculinity—as
something particularly quiet. But as much as you expect the
big, booming arrival of the planet's retrograde effects, its retrograde
period is actually quite sneaky. It creeps up on you when you least
expect it, and then suddenly, BAM! Your world is a disaster.

This combination of booming and sneakiness is what gives Mars the
reputation for having the most challenging retrograde period. Mars
retrograde attempts to teach us patience, a virtue that's not many
people's favorite. Mars is a planet of action, and when it's retrograde,
we get *in*action. We struggle with motivation and find ourselves bogged
down with distractions or lack of action when we try to express our
emotions, create anything, or really do anything that takes some effort.

"For this reason and how often it occurs," Atlas says, "I would say Mars
retrograde is the most challenging…[W]e live in a world that values
assertion and productivity, both of which are tempered during Mars
retrograde, which lasts longer than other inner planet retrogrades."

We should instead be taking the time to try to slow down. If you know
Mars is rife with tension, then use the retrograde period to diffuse
some of that. Embrace a slower lifestyle for a little while. And don't
work on any new or major projects as they likely will be a bit more

complicated than you expect. It's better to work on things that will give support to what you want to do once the retrograde period is over, like researching your options or weighing the pros and cons of each.

We saw a great example of this the fall after the COVID-19 pandemic rules were lifted. Mars went retrograde on October 30, 2022, just before the start of the holiday season. All at once, everyone was raring to go.

"Since then people were like, alright, gear up for the holidays," Kurtz says. "COVID is over. We're going to go out, we're going to do all the things. We're going to hang out with all the families. Everyone was trying to go out into the real world again, wanting to catch up on all the lost time and spend all their energy."

But then Mars retrograde happened, blindsiding pretty much everybody.

Suddenly, everyone was burned out. Plans fell through. People got sick. It's possible there was anger, frustration, and conflict in your world because nothing was working out. Think about staff shortages. Everyone was all ramped up to go back out to eat, but restaurants couldn't provide their typical level of service because there weren't enough employees. It was frustrating, and powerful Mars made it easier for us to get into little fights or to lash out at someone who didn't deserve it.

"The whole thing about Mars retrograde is to really question how you are spending your energy," Kurtz says. "Which battles are worth fighting, and which ones are just not worth your time?"

And indeed, this retrograde period can be a good time to actually reflect on the choices that have led you where you are. We don't like stopping to reflect on our past, we'd rather just move forward—but it's important to take a beat and determine if you're actually making the right decision about *how* to move forward.

Now look, Mars may be the worst retrograde period, but it doesn't mean your life is going to blow up right in front of you.

"I can't imagine that just because Mars goes retrograde, for example, a surgeon's skills somehow desert them," Wilkinson says. "Even with the Mars retrograde, your life is still moving forward. You just have to do other things that will support the main play after the retrograde. To defer is not to abandon. Sometimes in life, you can only just go as far as you can go."

It's like driving up to a *ROAD CLOSED* sign. You will still get to your destination, but there's a detour you need to figure out first. It's not like the road simply ceases to exist. It's just impossible to move forward until you figure out the *right way* to move forward—whether that means taking the detour or staying where you are to enjoy yourself until the road reopens. (Though, I don't really suggest the latter if there's not, you know, a place to stay, something to eat, and things to do. Otherwise you're just sitting in your car.)

The same goes for relationships between you and your family and friends. If someone's been holding a grudge, it can come out during this retrograde period. And then the involved parties can deal with it. They can get everything out in the open and think about resolutions.

Aside from the personal impact Mars retrograde has, it also has an impact on the world at large—especially an entire country's ability to defend itself. According to Madeline Gerwick, astrologer and owner of Polaris Business Guides, a company that focuses on astrology for businesses, Mars and Saturn represent the military. When Mars goes retrograde, she says, it's time for the military to think about how to shore up defenses and how to ensure the armed forces are in good enough shape to be able to defend a country's citizens should someone attack.

"Mars retrograde is oftentimes associated with war," Gerwick says. "It's also associated with picking up the rug and [confronting] all the things that were swept under the rug and never handled. All those things come to the forefront."

## Mars in the Business World

There's a saying in the astrological business world: millionaires don't have astrologers but billionaires do. It speaks to the need to create a plan, to meet retrogrades head on with a well-formed strategy. And for those of us with businesses, Mars retrograde in particular is the one we most need to watch out for, according to Gerwick. The retrograde comes around every two years and can really take business owners by surprise if they're not prepared.

"[Mars retrograde] is a process, and it's not always that much fun," she says. "But it can be very, very valuable, because you're setting yourself up for what you're going to do for the next two years. That's why it's such an important cycle."

Gerwick says most business owners create a one-year plan and a five-year plan. But the Mars retrograde cycle encourages them to plan every two years to coincide with what could happen during that backward motion.

Here's a great example. In the late 1990s, Alan Mulally was president of Boeing Commercial Airplanes. The company decided at that time to release a new aircraft—right in the middle of a Mars retrograde. Imagine their surprise when all the company VIPs got up in the air on the brand-new plane, and all the oxygen masks came down. The plane had to make an emergency landing in order to fix the problem.

Three weeks later, Mulally and his Boeing buddies were heading back up into the air with that same new plane and all the same VIPs. And guess what happened? The oxygen masks came down *again*. They had to land the plane and fix the problem *again*. Without prior knowledge of what was happening with the planets, Mulally looked, well, kind of like an idiot with a broken plane.

Fast forward to 2006, and Mulally had switched jobs. He was now the CEO of Ford Motor Company. And pretty quickly after he started working there, Mars went into retrograde. That poor man! Except this time, he'd learned his lesson. He'd made a two-year strategic plan that coincided with Mars retrograde. With that plan in action, Ford became the only car company out of the top three not to need a bailout from the government in 2008.

As Gerwick advises, if you own a business, a Mars retrograde is the time to really consider which markets you want to focus on for the next two years. Where can you compete the best? Where are you strongest?

Just be sure not to make any major decisions about the company during this period. Mars retrograde is not the best time to introduce new aspects of your business (as the Boeing snafu clearly shows).

"Whenever [Mars] is retrograde," Gerwick says, "it's really not a good time to, say, introduce a new product or start a new company because that would suggest that the company is either doing things it shouldn't be doing or it's incompetent. So, not a really good situation."

## Ritual for Mars Retrograde

During Mars retrograde, you'll notice everything starts to move at an…excessively…slow…pace. Projects lose steam, you lose patience, and any energy you had coming into this period slides swiftly into burnout. That's because Mars prefers to wreak havoc on productivity and energy levels. Thinking about starting a new hobby or business venture? Do yourself a favor and wait until Mars is back to direct transit. This slower period is a great opportunity to examine what choices you made to get where you are and where you want to be in the future.

# WHERE I'VE BEEN, WHERE I'M GOING

**YOU'LL NEED:**

A notebook

A highlighter

A pen

**DIRECTIONS:**

1. Open your notebook to a blank spread of pages. Atop the left page, write "Where I've Been." Atop the right page, write "Where I'm Going."

2. Start on the left. Under the heading, write a quick synopsis of where you're at in life right now. This could include anything you feel is pertinent, like where you live, your job, your income, and whom you're friends with.

3. Below the synopsis of your current world, write "How I Got Here." In this section, you should make a list of every choice you made to get to where you are now. Did you decide to sell your home or end a relationship? Or maybe both? Write those down. You want to be able to see the progression of events that led to your present life. If you need more space for this, flip the page and continue writing on the other side.

4. On the right-hand page, under "Where I'm Going," write a visionary statement of where you want to be in five years. It could be anything you want to achieve, but distill it down to an elevator pitch. Think something like this: "I want to own my home and have two children and a dog. I plan to be a C-suite level executive in my company." Tailor it to your hopes and dreams.

5. Under your elevator pitch, write the heading "How to Get Here." In this section, think about what steps you need to take to reach this goal. If it's to be a C-suite level exec, maybe you need to ask for a raise, more responsibility, or a promotion. If you want to own a home, your steps could be to determine where you want to buy a place and what your ideal property has. If you need

more space for this, flip the page and continue writing on the other side.

6. Take your highlighter and look through everything you've written. Highlight the five biggest choices you made to get where you are now, and the five steps you can give yourself a deadline for to get where you want to be. Examine the before and after, and see how they compare. How could the choices you made have been better? What can you do to use that experience to accomplish your future steps?

7. Write due dates next to your five actionable steps. Be specific. Don't just write "within two years." Write the exact date two years from now. Put those due dates in your calendar to encourage yourself to reach them.

8. As you move forward into the future, take notes in this same notebook about what you accomplish each month to reach your goals.

## Retrograde Review: Mars

- **Frequency of retrograde:** Every two years

- **Retrograde tendencies:**

  » *Positive:* Helps with patience, problem-solving

  » *Negative:* May prompt inaction, distraction, lack of productivity

- Get ready for everything to slow way down. This retrograde period brings inaction, delays, and obstacles to getting things done. But it helps us to learn that greatest of all the virtues: patience. It also encourages us to figure out our problems, especially any that were ignored or avoided, like a grudge between friends.

# Chapter 8

# JUPITER

Remember during the COVID-19 pandemic, when every store started to run out of toilet paper? Shops had limits on how much you could buy, and we all had to be economical with our usage at home. It was kind of a pain, and we can partially thank Jupiter's retrograde cycle for it.

Jupiter represents expansion. So, it makes sense that when it retrogrades, there's a loss of something or not enough of things we need (like flour—remember that from the pandemic?). Jupiter's retrograde period turns our experience of the planet into a contraction.

That being said, it's thankfully not always that difficult for us, and it really only retrogrades once a year. Jupiter also represents opportunity, vision, inspiration, and the ability to take a leap of faith. We want to grab opportunities and have a great time, thanks to the planet. The retrograde is a time to look within.

A few of the astrologers interviewed for this book note that Jupiter is one of the easier retrograde periods. You may feel unlucky and small for a little bit of it, but overall, it's not as likely to affect you on a super personal level.

"Jupiter is an auspicious planet, and its retrograde is characterized by turning our outward expansion inward to work on ourselves, scale back, and integrate all of the lessons we collected externally over the last eight months," Atlas says. "Since the nature of Jupiter is less destructive than some of the other outer planets, this period is usually pretty easy to navigate. [It] can help you grow internally and emerge with a new mindset by the end of the retrograde period."

Plus, just because Jupiter as a whole rules luck and success, that doesn't mean the retrograde period is going to bring the opposite of luck and success. It's likely to affect you in other ways, like helping you learn about past opportunities that had to be delayed because you hadn't learned everything you needed to know yet to traverse that time in your life. And you may need to revisit your sense of identity in its entirety to accomplish that task.

"With Jupiter retrograde, there's more of a review of what we consider to be truth," Allemana says. "That can be challenging for people, especially if you have really strong ideologies that you're really attached to. When they're challenged on that, it can be a threat to their own sense of identity. But if we're relatively fluid with our opinions and what we think is true and morally right, …we can be a little more fluid in order to have a greater embracing of other points of view and other people and other situations."

Jupiter's retrograde period comes down to our individual spiritual journeys. It gives us a chance to embrace life and the world as they are, rather than trying to fix them to fit into our views of what we want them to be.

That doesn't mean it's a bad idea to have lofty goals about how we want to change the world, of course. Instead, we should embrace the expansion aspect of the planet and learn to bring new ideas in and build off of those.

"[It's] connected to this idea that we want to expand what we can accept into our field of view because the world is the way it is and it doesn't make sense to reject it," Allemana says. "But we can embrace it and say, 'OK, that needs to be changed.' That's really where the challenge of Jupiter retrograde is, to challenge us to expand our perspectives and accept truths that are different than ours, while also knowing and honoring what our truth is."

## Ritual for Jupiter Retrograde

Jupiter rules luck, success, and achievement. But that's not what we're going to focus on in this retrograde ritual. Instead, you're going to take a big step forward to get there by expanding your mind. When Jupiter turns retrograde, it's a sign for you to take a step outside your own box and really evaluate your beliefs in life. You can't improve if you're always stuck in the same mindset.

# EXPAND YOUR MIND CRYSTAL GRID

**YOU'LL NEED:**

A small photo of you

Small photos of five people you've recently disagreed with

1 crystal you feel best represents you

1 selenite for clarity

1 rose quartz for universal love

1 amethyst for patience

1 tiger's-eye for protection

1 lapis lazuli for wisdom

1 orange highlighter

**DIRECTIONS:**

1. Place the photo of you on a flat surface. Arrange the five other photos around it in a pentagon shape, so you could draw a five-pointed star with them as the points.

2. Place the crystal that represents you on your photo.

3. Place the other crystals on the other photos. Rely on your intuition to determine which crystal to place on which photo.

4. Meditate on the grid you've made. Focus on each person's photo and think about your recent disagreements. Consider what you didn't agree with and try to put yourself in their shoes and see it from their point of view. Once you reach that point, imagine the crystal glowing a bright white. Keep it glowing in your mind's eye as you move to the next person.

5. Once you've finished meditating on the grid and can visualize all the crystals except yours glowing bright, pick up the highlighter. Hold it out as a wand and trace a star through all five points. Imagine you're leaving a shining trail of orange connecting the crystals as you move along.

6. When you can see the shining star and glowing crystals in your mind, take the highlighter and trace a spiral path from each stone around and into your picture. With each stone that connects to yours, your own crystal begins to shine brighter.

Continue until you've connected all the crystals to yours and all are equally bright in your mind.

7.  Take a deep breath in. As you do so, imagine your crystal glowing brighter than the others. Take three more deep breaths. After each one, whisper, "We are all doing the best we can." After you've whispered it three times, still your mind and say at full voice, "I understand."

8.  Leave the crystal grid up overnight. The next morning, gather the crystals and leave them in the sunlight for an hour, then return them to their regular storage place.

## Retrograde Review: Jupiter

- **Frequency of retrograde:** Once a year

- **Retrograde tendencies:**

  » *Positive:* Supports opportunity, inspiration, faith

  » *Negative:* May trigger loss, shortages, threats to our sense of identity

- Jupiter's retrograde brings contraction, the opposite of expansion, so expect to see shortages or loss of some kind on a national or global level. Counteract that by embracing the planet's overall sense of expansion to be inspired to try and believe new things.

# Chapter 9

# SATURN

O ut of all the planets with rings, Saturn's are the biggest and brightest. They are the most visible rings of the outer planets. From our view, it looks like Saturn is contained, restrained from reaching out into the universe. And astrologically, that's exactly what's happening.

Saturn is the planet of discipline, restriction, and limitation. (It's those rings kicking in!) So when it goes retrograde, it really just brings *more* discipline, restriction, and limitation—just in a different way. You may have some issues with authority and structure during this retrograde period, or you may discover you need to change some sort of process you've been doing. And it's not just you, either. Since Saturn is considered one of the social planets, the retrograde results can affect a lot of people.

That can be reflected in policy or government changes. The head honchos may have made a decision or a promise, but suddenly they're going back on that decision, trying to reverse it or looking for a way to do it differently.

A great example of this? Roe v. Wade. The landmark ruling was over-turned during a Saturn retrograde.

"It's things like that, where a lot of the time, there is a marked back-tracking," Oliver says. "Especially on the collective level, because Saturn is mostly concerned with the collective, like going back and saying, Alright, you know what? We need to reestablish different ways of being rather than go on with the same methodology that we've been using so far."

That doesn't necessarily mean the changes will be bad, like the chaos we've seen that's ensued since the repeal of Roe v. Wade. The back-tracking may be something good, like reversing a law that ended up doing more harm than good.

For individuals during a Saturn retrograde, it's important to take a deeper look at your own discipline, restrictions, and limitations. You may find that you didn't set clear enough boundaries and someone took advantage of your kindness. Or maybe you slacked on your responsibilities more than you should have. This retrograde period—which lasts for about four months every year—is a catalyst to push you to rethink your actions.

And that's why Wilkinson, for one, thinks Saturn retrogrades are a wonderful thing.

"Saturn is the understanding that leads you to wisdom," he says. "Sometimes we need to review the material. That being the case, thank heaven we don't have to master everything the first time. We actually get cut some slack where we get to slow down, get to take a look at things. We get to make sure that we heard it and saw it and understood it correctly. Then we move on with it."

## Ritual for Saturn Retrograde

Nobody likes a bad habit. It's always there, lurking around the corner, waiting for you to slip up and indulge once more in the thrill of doing something you shouldn't. Until you break that habit, that is. But it's not that easy. A study from the *European Journal of Social Psychology* found that breaking a bad habit can take anywhere from 18 days to a mind-numbing 254 days. For as long as it takes, sometimes it seems like Saturn—the planet that rules the building blocks of good habits in the form of discipline, karma, and wisdom—has just left us in the dust to deal with our problems alone. But when retrograde comes around, it's a great time to face (and get rid of) the vices we've been neglecting to address.

# STOMPING OUT BAD HABITS

**YOU'LL NEED:**

A piece of notebook paper

Scissors

A green marker or crayon

Double-sided tape

A comfortable pair
of flat shoes

An evening out with friends

**DIRECTIONS:**

1. Cut two squares out of the notebook paper. Be sure they're smaller than the heel of your shoes.

2. Using the green marker or crayon, write the bad habit you wish to break onto the slips of paper. If you have two bad habits you'd like to break, write one on each piece of paper.

3. Tape the papers to the bottom of your shoes, one piece per shoe.

4. Put on the shoes and go out with your friends for the night. Every step you take will be another step toward breaking your bad habits. Try not to come home until the papers are gone or destroyed.

# Retrograde Review: Saturn

- **Frequency of retrograde:** Every 12 months

- **Retrograde tendencies:**

  » *Positive:* Allows for rethinking your actions, breaking bad habits; may trigger process changes that affect a lot of people

  » *Negative:* May cause difficulties with discipline, authority, restriction, and structure, as well as spurring process changes that affect a lot of people

- Saturn rules discipline, authority, and structure. So when it retrogrades, we'll naturally struggle with all of those. Take the time to rethink how you've acted in the past or how you're acting now and see what you can do to break the bad habits that are causing you to struggle with discipline and authority. Also, expect some major procedural changes that will affect a large group of people, like the change of a long-held law.

# Chapter 10

# URANUS

U ranus has been a rebel from the start. When it was first discovered in 1781, humankind was all atwitter with the shock of a new planet reforming the cosmos. Imagine everyone's surprise when we learned that Uranus has a feature that makes it completely unique from all other planets: it rotates horizontally rather than vertically like its celestial friends. If Uranus were a person, it would be that bad boy greaser in your math class who sketches instead of calculates.

Uranus is radical, independent, and revolutionary. Astrologers interviewed for this book describe its retrograde both as their favorite and one of the most difficult. And that's because it has a tendency to shake things up.

"Uranus retrograde is my favorite because it represents uniqueness, individuality, eccentricity, and evolutionary (and revolutionary) movements," King says. "Another annual retrograde, spending five months a year in reverse motion, this planet is a generational planet and tends to oscillate back and forth to generate all the new, first-time, and shock-and-awe progress of the world through genius ideas, creations, and advances."

People with heavy Uranus influences yearn to be out on their own, maybe working in a freelance career where they don't have to report to anyone but themselves. They're changemakers, not afraid to pivot things to a horizontal axis instead of a vertical one (See what I did there?), and are generally welcoming of change.

It is possible, though, that the need to have freedom and change and excitement could mean that in your subconscious, you're looking for a fresh start. Maybe you feel stagnant or confined and want to break free. When Uranus goes retrograde, it can intensify those feelings. If you feel aligned to that energy of breaking free from the past, that can be a pretty liberating experience because it allows you to do just that. But if you're like most people, you might be in opposition to Uranus's energy—meaning stuck in your own patterns, with a little too much order and structure, which makes you feel like life is calcifying in front of you.

"Uranus is the planet that comes in and breaks all that up," Allemana says. "It sets off a bomb and says, 'No, that doesn't fit for you anymore. You need to grow beyond that.' So Uranus's function is to stimulate new creative energy to blast an obstacle out of the way. And it might be an obstacle you're really attached to and don't want to let go of, but that's actually limiting your growth and your potential and your freedom....It can seem really disruptive."

And it's not just on the personal level. When Uranus goes retrograde, things heat up on the global scale as well. Think political and social issues, which can get a bit bonkers during that time. If you see something truly unpleasant happening in the world, it's very possible we're going through a Uranus retrograde transit at the time. That's what Uranus does to us. It shows up suddenly and causes a lot of disruption. And since the planet is directly linked to the collective social dynamic and issues at large, the changes it brings can be awfully complicated to manage and integrate into society.

# Ritual for Uranus Retrograde

It's probably safe to say that we all remember a time when we were growing up that we yearned for freedom, to break out of the (clearly tyrannical) rule of our guardians and find our own selves out there in the world. Well, that's Uranus for you. The planet represents creativity and individuality—all the things that make us who we are. When Uranus is retrograde, it's important to take stock of our personalities and ensure we're living our best lives. And a fun way to do that is by getting creative in the kitchen with a color-changing tea ritual.

# CREATIVE INDIVIDUALITEA

**YOU'LL NEED:**

A teakettle (or microwave)     A tea bag or steeper

A clear glass mug              Half a lemon

1.5 teaspoons loose           Honey, to taste
butterfly pea flower tea

**DIRECTIONS:**

1. Lay out all your materials on the counter in your kitchen. Meditate on them for a moment and then look inward, focusing on a feeling of self-love.

2. Fill your teakettle and set it to boil. (If you don't have a teakettle, fill your mug with water and microwave it for 1.5 to 2 minutes.)

3. Place the butterfly pea flower tea into the tea bag or steeper. Put it in your mug.

4. When the water is hot, pour it slowly into your mug. Watch the blue tendrils swirl up from the tea. Imagine those are strands of your favorite personality traits reaching out from your body to make themselves known. Let the tea steep, covered, for up to five minutes.

5. When the water is sufficiently blue, remove the tea bag. Squeeze the juice from half a lemon into the cup while stirring. You'll see the tea turn purple. Meditate on the color change for a moment. Hold the mug up to your nose and take a deep breath in.

6. Add honey to taste. As you drink the tea, imagine the creativity of the purple reaching down into your belly and blossoming into new ideas.

# Retrograde Review: Uranus

- **Frequency of retrograde:** Once every 12 months

- **Retrograde tendencies:**

  » *Positive:* Supports uniqueness, individuality, progress, revolution

  » *Negative:* Influences mass social and political change

- Uranus retrograde shows up unexpectedly with a big plan to shake things up in society. Expect radical thoughts, evolution, and revolution. You can break free from the past during this retrograde period—which can be difficult because you may not want to change the way you've always done things. But if you allow yourself to be moved by Uranus retrograde, you may discover a whole new world of fun and unique things about yourself.

# Chapter 11

# NEPTUNE

If you've been waiting for the easiest retrograde period, surprise! It's just arrived. Astrologers interviewed for this book generally agree that Neptune retrograde is one we don't feel as much—and one dealing with spiritual lessons we've been trying to learn our whole lives, so we are familiar with the energy.

Astronomically, there's a simple reason Neptune retrograde has the least effect: it's so far away. Out of all the planetary bodies that astronomy recognizes as planets, Neptune is dead last. It's the farthest out. That means we see it retrograde for just over five months at a time, the second longest compared to Pluto (if you consider Pluto a planet).

Astrologically speaking, Neptune isn't as personal as one of the more devastating planets in retrograde. This planet focuses on dreams, imagination, and intuition, as well as the drive to move into the ethereal world. And that's not really stuff that's going to impact us too heavily on the day-to-day, like something revolving around communication and interpersonal relations would. To be honest, sometimes we're not even aware that Neptune is retrograding at all. It can be a little secretive.

"I don't seem to notice major issues that arise through Neptune retrograde, although that's kind of Neptune's nature," Allemana says. "It's kind of hidden, and you really have to look and blur things to really see how Neptune is operating."

That's because the issues that come up during Neptune retrograde are spiritual lessons we've already seen, but we're continuing to learn. At this point, we know how the world is working, and we know we can't change it or reject it—or at least it doesn't make sense to do so. Instead, it's a time of expanding what you accept into your field of view, opening your mind to new ideas and really diving into your creativity and imagination, which may seem like it's deserted you a bit.

In her book *Astrology: Using the Wisdom of the Stars in Your Everyday Life*, author Carole Taylor says that during a direct transit, we go deep into our imagination.

"Neptune distorts reality enough for us to slip through into a more fantastical frame of mind, and any planets or angles that Neptune is in aspect to will be seen through the lens of your imagination and be swept up into a dream or romance," Taylor writes.

So when it goes retrograde, we might find life just a little bit more dull. Maybe your dreams get more strange and vivid, or you get writer's block, or you have a creative lull.

Now is the time to lean into that aspect of your personality and really dissect what might be holding you back.

## Ritual for Neptune Retrograde

Have you ever met someone and just known that they would be your friend? You could practically see yourselves ten years down the line, hanging out and swapping secrets and inside jokes. How many times has that vision come true? Intuition is a powerful thing, alerting us to new friends, yes, but also helping us to decipher things we don't fully understand, warning us away from situations that might be dangerous, and giving us a heads-up when things might be a major success or go sour. Sometimes, though, we lose track of that quirk.

Neptune represents dreams, subconscious, and precognition. Spend this retrograde period rediscovering your ability to listen to your gut.

# INTUITIVE SELF-HYPNOSIS

**YOU'LL NEED:**

Just yourself and
a comfy bed!

**DIRECTIONS:**

1.  Start by meditating on a problem you've been experiencing that needs solving, or a decision you've been struggling to make. Tell yourself that today, you will have your answer. Repeat this to the point that you believe it.

2.  Lay down on your back in bed. Be sure the room is quiet. Give yourself a few minutes to get comfortable.

3.  Close your eyes and take several deep breaths, in through your nose and out through your mouth. With each exhale, feel yourself sinking deeper and deeper into the comfort of the bed.

4.  In your mind's eye, picture a staircase. With each breath you take, feel the staircase becoming more real. Imagine the hardness of the staircase beneath your feet, the width and depth of the steps.

5.  In your mind's eye, begin to walk up the staircase, slowly. Take a new step with each breath. Think about your problem or decision as you ascend.

6.  As you reach the midway point of the staircase, imagine a door appearing at the top. Remind yourself that the answer you're seeking is just beyond that door.

7.  Keep climbing until you reach the door. If you don't feel ready to open it, keep climbing. Once you get there, open the door. Your answer will be on the other side.

8.  Slowly start to wiggle your hands and feet, coming out of the meditation. Immediately write down what you saw and see where it leads you.

# Retrograde Review: Neptune

- **Frequency of retrograde:** Once a year

- **Retrograde tendencies:**

  » *Positive:* Supports intuition, dreams, with little impact on personal life

  » *Negative:* May cause creative blocks, muddled intuition, a feeling that things are dull

- We feel Neptune's retrograde the least of all the retrogrades because the planet is so far out. You may feel a lull in your daily life or creative mind during this time; take the retrograde period as a sign to dive into that aspect of your personality.

# Chapter 12

# WHAT ABOUT PLUTO?

P oor Pluto. It was a planet, then it wasn't, then maybe it was again…and now it seems like no one ever really knows for sure, except for astronomers.

The whole situation is understandably confusing. Pluto is considered a dwarf planet now—demoted from its past as the ninth major planet, situated the farthest from the sun. And according to the International Astronomical Union (IAU), the group of scientists that decides which planets actually get that classification, dwarf planets aren't technically planets.

In order for a celestial body to be considered a major planet in our solar system, it has to meet three criteria. First, it has to orbit around the sun. (Score—Pluto: 1, IAU: 0.) Second, it must be large enough that gravitational forces determine the shape, making it round or nearly round. (Score—Pluto: 2, IAU: 0.) Third, it has to have strong enough gravity to "clear out its neighborhood," the IAU says. That means that the gravitational pull of the planet has led to it absorbing the stuff in space around its orbit, like asteroids and other space rocks. Unfortunately, Pluto hasn't done that. It's still surrounded by comets, asteroids, plutinos, and other objects floating around its Kuiper Belt home. (Score—Pluto: 2, IAU: 1. Dang.)

So, Pluto doesn't make the cut. It was downgraded from a major planet on August 24, 2006. Some sentimental scientists and astronomy fans still mourn that moment, though, and honor its demotion every August 24 in a holiday aptly named Pluto Demoted Day. To be fair, it was a pretty historic moment, and it's not like Pluto is any less interesting than it was before.

For those of you pining for the past days of Pluto planet-hood, all is not lost. Just look to astrology, a field where Pluto is still considered a planet.

"In astrology, every object moving in the celestial sphere or through the zodiac is a planet," Allemana says. "The only exceptions, although these terms aren't held to very strictly, are the sun and the moon. They are considered luminaries and aren't really planets, astrologically speaking. But they're still often referred to as planets. Any wandering object through the sky is considered a planet."

And just like the other planets, Pluto goes retrograde. It only happens once a year, but when it does, it stays retrograde for five to six months before returning direct. Pluto rules the subconscious—sex, death, rebirth, and power—and it's not messing around. This planet's retrograde is intense.

"Pluto is like the magma under a volcano," Allemana says. "There's a lot of energy and power there, but you don't see it until it bursts, and then it's very transformative and can be very destructive."

When you consider that the 2011 earthquake and tsunami in Japan happened just before Pluto retrograde; the Boston Marathon bombing happened just as Pluto was turning retrograde; and the planet itself is nicknamed "The Great Destroyer," Pluto's intensity might make more sense.

It's partially because of Pluto's energy. It's far away from us, and that's mirrored in how easily we see its effects in our worlds. Pluto reaches deep into the subconscious and manipulates us on that level. We don't notice it in our moment-to-moment consciousness, at least not until something forces us to. Think of it as working within your shadow self—the part of your personality that you don't acknowledge on a regular basis, the part that brings your self-perceived negative qualities to light, like laziness, depression, and greed. Once something triggers that part of you, like a frustrating situation, you see it come out in full force.

That doesn't mean your shadow self is bad and should be ignored, though. And neither should Pluto retrograde and how you react to it. You should use that energy to your advantage because you still have those spiritual lessons to master. It's a continual transformation.

"When Pluto's retrograde, there's a call to look deep within ourselves, to look a little deeper into our own shadow," Allemana says. "Look at where our tendencies are to take something for ourselves or to desire power for ourselves, in whatever ways it might show up for us. And then, try and work with that and incorporate that into your daily life."

You might think of those tendencies as bad, evil, negative, or dysfunctional. But that's only because you're not conscious of them and how they're working within you. In reality, they aren't bad. They're just another part of your personality to explore. And you can't truly know yourself unless you learn about all of yourself, rather than stuffing some things under the rug. So, embrace that anger, that envy, that desire to be a little mean sometimes. Once you accept these tendencies, you can put them to use in better ways in your life.

"On an ideal level, if we're all paying attention to when Pluto goes retrograde, this is a good period," Allemana says. "Pluto retrograde is really that process of looking deep within and incorporating what we find. Pluto's a very slow-moving planet because it's so far out there. It's operating very slowly and subtly, but very powerfully."

# Ritual for Pluto Retrograde

Since Pluto retrograde works on a subconscious level, this ritual is focused on exploring that part of your personality. You'll work to discover what's hiding in your shadow self, begin to embrace it, and learn to use it to your advantage. The retrograde energy will make the whole process clearer for you.

# EMBRACING YOUR SHADOW SELF

**YOU'LL NEED:**

A quiet place to sit alone for 20 to 30 minutes

1 piece of selenite

1 piece of onyx

1 piece of smoky quartz

1 piece of lapis lazuli

A blank piece of unlined paper

A set of crayons (the amount and colors are up to you)

**DIRECTIONS:**

1. Find a place where you can sit undisturbed, either on the ground or at a table.

2. Arrange the crystals around you in any order, with one in each of the cardinal directions. If you're sitting at a desk, place the crystals on the desk, one in each of the cardinal directions.

3. Place the paper and the crayons in front of you.

4. Take a few minutes to ground yourself. Close your eyes and take a few deep breaths, slowly and steadily. As you're breathing, picture roots growing beneath you and a treetop growing above you. With each breath in, the roots and treetop get longer. When you're calm and feeling centered, open your eyes.

5. Now, think about the person who upset you the most over the last week, whether that means they made you sad, angry, uncomfortable, or any other strong emotion you perceived as negative. Focus on them for several minutes, feeling the same things you felt at that time.

6. Pick up the crayons and draw how you feel. You can draw anything, in any color, as long as it represents that person and your resulting emotions. It could be something as detailed as a portrait of them or you, or even just a harsh red scribble across the page. Get creative while you relive your feelings on the page.

7. When you've finished your drawing, spend some time examining it and trying to understand what led you to feel the way you

did. Were you triggered by something they said or did? Was something negative in your past rehashed by their behavior? Did they have a personality that rubbed you the wrong way? Really think about what exactly led to those emotions.

8. Once you have a handle on why you felt how you felt, put both hands on the drawing. Stare directly at it and firmly say, "My emotions are valid. I accept and love all aspects of my truth. I am not ashamed." Repeat as many times as you feel necessary.

9. Close your eyes and take several slow deep breaths to return to your everyday world. Do what you'd like with your artwork; frame it and hang it, keep it in a folder, throw it away—it's up to you. But don't forget the exercise and what you produced. Move forward with deeper knowledge of your darker feelings.

# Retrograde Review: Pluto

- **Frequency of retrograde:** Once a year

- **Retrograde tendencies:**

  » *Positive:* Allows for transformation, acceptance of the shadow self

  » *Negative:* Influences destruction

- Pluto retrograde has a destructive energy that seems like it brings all of your bad qualities out in full force. But it's actually a chance to connect with those energies you perceive as negative and give yourself an opportunity to learn why they're important.

# Chapter 13

# CHIRON WHO?

J ust when you thought you knew all the planets, along comes Chiron. Well, OK, Chiron isn't *exactly* a full-blown planet. It's considered a minor planet, roaming around the outer solar system between Saturn and Uranus. Scientifically, it's considered a comet or asteroid as well as a minor planet.

You may not know about Chiron, and that's for good reasons. The asteroid wasn't discovered until 1977, and it's pretty small, much smaller than the other planets in our solar system. Astrologically speaking, though, it has a unique symbolism that pulls together personal, collective, social, and ancestral themes from throughout the zodiac.

To understand Chiron properly, we first need to get to know a group of centaurs in Greek mythology. Centaurs are half man, half horse. They were born out of a union between Ixion (a guest in Olympus who tried to seduce Hera, Zeus's wife) and Nephele (a cloud nymph Zeus formed to trick Ixion). The mythological centaur race was lusty, violent, and uncultured.

Chiron, though, was the exact opposite of most centaurs. He was indeed half horse, half man, but instead of having a wild streak, he was calm, intelligent, and kind. As he grew, he became a gifted healer and teacher, skilled in music and poetry. He was a musician, a mentor, and a prophet.

So why the difference? Well, Chiron wasn't really related to the centaurs. His father was the pre-Olympian god Cronus, who impregnated the water nymph Philyra while he was in the form of a horse. But Philyra and Cronus didn't want Chiron when he was born (apparently he looked…too much like a horse), and they immediately abandoned him. The Greek god Apollo found him and decided to become his foster father. As dad, Apollo introduced Chiron to all sorts of things: lyres, archery, medicine, poetry, and more. According to some mythologists, Chiron invented the art of healing thanks to this upbringing.

Unfortunately, Chiron wasn't really able to heal himself. During a riotous moment fueled by wine gifted from Dionysus, Chiron was accidentally shot with a poison-tipped arrow. He couldn't do anything about it, and the pain got worse and worse. So, instead of living that way, Chiron gave up his immortality to secure freedom for Prometheus, the god of fire, who was being punished for eternity for giving fire to humanity. Prometheus was freed, and Chiron was placed into the universe as the constellation Centaurus.

You can probably see now why Chiron is considered the Wounded Healer. The poor guy just wanted to spread love and health, and instead he was poisoned, then abandoned. Luckily for us, though, we get to embrace Chiron every year when the asteroid/mini-planet/comet/(Just make a decision, science!), goes retrograde. And Chiron is retrograde a lot: at least once a year for about five months at a time. Its orbit is unstable and a little weird, though, crossing the path of Saturn and getting awfully close to Uranus.

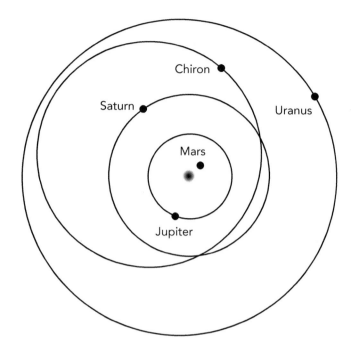

Chiron is the most popular non-planet planet to work with among astrologers, particularly because its weird orbit makes it stay in some zodiac signs much longer than others. As of this writing, Chiron is going through Aries, and it'll stay in Aries for about nine to eleven years. It will only stay in some other signs, though, for around two years. That time difference is solely related to the orbit, however, and not because of the retrograde period.

Depending on whom you ask, Chiron's retrograde movement either has a smallish effect on us or a major effect. It has a tendency to allow old wounds from our lives (or past lives!) to resurface, giving us the chance to deal with these very specific pain points.

"I use myself as an example," Salomon says. "My Chiron is in Gemini [in my birth chart]. I've always been kind of quirky and weird, and my fear or my wounding has always been in how people understand me. Because it's in Gemini, it's a communication thing. They don't understand me."

So when Chiron goes retrograde, it actually gives her a bit of a release. She's a bit more self-confident with communication and has the time to deal with any communication blocks. But for others, like for someone who feels wounded from a past full of infertility problems, Chiron moving retrograde might make that emotional pain more acute. And that means that it's time to come to terms with that issue.

## Ritual for Chiron Retrograde

Oh gosh, don't you just *love* digging up past trauma? Well, get ready to do it when Chiron goes retrograde. It helps to keep in mind that Chiron is also called the Wounded Healer. That should clue you in to what you're about to experience. Luckily, though, with the resurfacing of trauma comes healing. Take this time to look inward and work with those past pains to become a more whole person moving forward. Oh, and bonus, you get to do this in the bath. Because what's more healing than a candlelit evening in the tub?

# HEALING RITUAL BATH

**YOU'LL NEED:**

1 cup lavender-scented Epsom salts

Your favorite bubble bath

As many tealights as you want to fill up your bathroom, in your favorite colors

A handful of dried chamomile

A handful of dried mint

A handful of fresh rose petals

A handful of dried eucalyptus

**DIRECTIONS:**

1. Draw a warm bath, first mixing in the Epsom salts and then mixing in the bubble bath.

2. While the tub is filling, put tealights all around your bathroom. Use enough to make a subtle and cozy glow with candles when the bathroom light is off. Place each candle with intention, picking a spot that feels good to you (and is, of course, safe).

3. Once the bath is ready, sprinkle on the handfuls of chamomile, mint, rose petals, and eucalyptus.

4. Get in the tub and relax. Soak in all the healing and loving powers of the plants in the bath with you. Think about how your past trauma has informed who you are today.

5. Take a moment to meditate on gratitude—not for the traumatizing event, but for the fact that you got past it and are better on the other side. Remind yourself that you can do anything, that you are strong, and that you can handle whatever comes your way.

6. Soak in the tub until you're ready to get out.

# Retrograde Review: Chiron

- **Frequency of retrograde:** Once a year

- **Retrograde tendencies:**

  » *Positive:* Gives us the chance to deal with trauma once and for all

  » *Negative:* Resurfaces old wounds

- Chiron is called the Wounded Healer and is an asteroid and a minor planet. It works its magic by bringing up past trauma and giving you the chance to resolve it. The retrograde may make this a more emotional process or a calmer process, depending on your personal astrology.

## Chapter 14

# RETROGRADE
# WRAP-UP

Alright! By now, you should have created your birth chart, learned where your own retrogrades are, and explored a bit about each retrograde and how to manage it. So, what next?

Well, the most important thing you can do next is *keep learning*. Retrogrades are complicated. You probably noticed how the astrologers interviewed for this book didn't always agree, right? That's because there are so many ways to interpret retrogrades based on any one person's particular astrology. So take the knowledge you gained and apply it to your own life, your own birth chart, your own path of moving forward. And then dive deeper! See where it takes you on your life's path.

One of the interesting things I've found about planetary retrogrades is that sometimes, it seems like you might vibe better with one than with the others. Pay attention to that feeling and investigate it. Most likely, you have some special connection to that planet in your personal astrology. Have a good look at your birth chart. What's in retrograde, and how do the planets interact with one another? If you look deep enough, you're likely to find your answer there.

For example, I've always felt a special connection to Venus and its retrograde periods. I've almost always been in relationships, and I prefer connecting with others on a deeper level. I even did a full report on the goddess Venus when I was in high school—go figure! If you want to go even more in-depth here, in the painting *The Birth of Venus*, the goddess is standing in a giant scallop shell. Well, I love scallops. I could eat them every day, given the chance. Sure, that connection is probably just a silly coincidence, but you never know.

Anyway—onto my personal astrology and how this connection to Venus relates to my life.

My Venus is retrograde in Virgo and it squares with Uranus retrograde. Remember, Venus rules relationships, and Virgo represents communication, development, and humility, among other things. Uranus, as we know, is independent and likes to shake things up. And with squared planets, tension is at a high between the two, causing a retrograde of at least one of them to be particularly tough.

When I extrapolate that information to my life, I can very clearly see the connections. Sure, I've always been in relationships, but they have a habit of ending a bit disastrously. (If you've been through a particularly contentious divorce, I see you—and me.) Communication has been a pretty consistent theme in those breakups; either one or both of us doesn't communicate in the best way for the relationship. And while I like being in relationships, I also desperately need my independence. That's why my day job is as a travel writer! I get to go out and explore a lot…and my partner has to stay at home taking care of the daily tasks, which can create some struggles at home.

Let's break it down further to add in the astrology. I've always been in relationships—that's Venus. But those relationships have ended poorly. Hello, Venus retrograde! Typically my relationship problems and tricky breakups are exacerbated by poor communication, welcoming the Venus retrograde in Virgo specifically to the picture.

And my independence (Uranus) can cause issues at home as well (Uranus retrograde).

So, now that I know all this information about my natal Venus and Uranus retrogrades, I can tell that when one (or both, why not?) of them comes around, it'll probably be a bit of a difficult period for me. Let's add in a Venus retrograde to see how it affected my life, based on my astrology.

In 2018, I got divorced. It was a tough one, with the worst part spreading from October to November. As it turns out, that exact period of time was a Venus retrograde. And not only did my relationship end poorly (Venus retrograde), it was made worse by the fact that my ex-husband had moved to another state (Uranus's independence) and didn't want to communicate (Virgo) with me to finish the divorce process.

Think of a particularly rough period in your life and Google the retrogrades for that time span. You might find some interesting connections, like I did.

I can work on making these retrograde periods better for me, though. During Venus retrograde, I now know I need to pay extra attention to my communication style with my new husband. I should also consider not traveling for work during the retrograde, since I know (thanks to my astrology) that the independence I seek might cause a problem.

Now that you know what it looks like practically to examine the relationships between your personal astrology, natal retrogrades, and your life, you should be able to use that information to help you handle any retrograde periods coming your way.

Retrogrades don't have to be stressful times. Now that you're armed with everything you've learned in this book, it's time to go forward and prosper.

# SECTION III

## RETROGRADE CALENDARS

## Chapter 15

# RETROGRADE CALENDARS THROUGH 2030

I f you really want to harness the power of planetary retrogrades, it's best to know exactly when they are, so you can plan in advance. Luckily, I'm taking care of that for you. The following calendars track the dates each planet goes into and out of retrograde, and the astrological sun signs each planet is leaving and entering—from 2024 to 2030. Use them as reference guides that you can come back to throughout the years. With these calendars, you'll never have to worry about being caught off guard.

An important note to remember: when retrogrades go in and out of certain zodiac signs, it doesn't have anything to do with your personal sun sign. A sun sign, which determines your zodiac sign at birth, only refers to the position of the sun when you were born and which zodiac constellation was hidden behind it. That constellation is your sun sign. Zodiac signs for retrogrades, rather, note what part of the zodiac the planet is in when it transits through.

Let's use the birthdate of August 13, 1983, as an example: The sun sign, or zodiac sign, is Leo. But on that date, Venus was retrograde in Virgo, and Uranus and Neptune were retrograde in Sagittarius.

If you see your birthday or zodiac sign listed for any of the retrogrades in these calendars, remember that it won't necessarily affect you worse than it will someone else.

# 2024

| PLANET | IN DATE | OUT DATE | ZODIAC IN | ZODIAC OUT |
|--------|---------|----------|-----------|------------|
| Mercury | December 13, 2023 | January 2, 2024 | Capricorn | Sagittarius |
| | April 1 | April 25 | Aries | Aries |
| | August 5 | August 28 | Virgo | Leo |
| | November 26 | December 15 | Sagittarius | Sagittarius |
| Venus | None | | | |
| Mars | December 6, 2024 | February 24, 2025 | Leo | Cancer |
| Jupiter | October 9, 2024 | February 4, 2025 | Gemini | Gemini |
| Saturn | June 29 | November 15 | Pisces | Pisces |
| Uranus | August 29, 2023 | January 27, 2024 | Taurus | Taurus |
| | September 1, 2024 | January 30, 2025 | Taurus | Taurus |
| Neptune | July 2 | December 7 | Pisces | Pisces |
| Pluto | May 2 | October 12 | Aquarius | Capricorn |
| Chiron | July 26 | December 29 | Aries | Aries |

# 2025

| PLANET | IN DATE | OUT DATE | ZODIAC IN | ZODIAC OUT |
|--------|---------|----------|-----------|------------|
| Mercury | March 15 | April 7 | Aries | Pisces |
| | July 18 | August 11 | Leo | Leo |
| | November 9 | November 29 | Sagittarius | Scorpio |
| Venus | March 2 | April 13 | Aries | Pisces |
| Mars | December 6, 2024 | February 24, 2025 | Leo | Cancer |
| Jupiter | October 9, 2024 | February 4, 2025 | Gemini | Gemini |
| | November 11, 2025 | March 11, 2026 | Cancer | Cancer |
| Saturn | July 13 | November 28 | Aries | Pisces |
| Uranus | September 1, 2024 | January 30, 2025 | Taurus | Taurus |
| | September 6, 2025 | February 4, 2026 | Gemini | Taurus |
| Neptune | July 4 | December 10 | Aries | Pisces |
| Pluto | May 4 | October 14 | Aquarius | Aquarius |
| Chiron | July 30, 2025 | January 2, 2026 | Aries | Aries |

# 2026

| PLANET | IN DATE | OUT DATE | ZODIAC IN | ZODIAC OUT |
|--------|---------|----------|-----------|------------|
| Mercury | February 26 | March 20 | Pisces | Pisces |
| | June 29 | July 23 | Cancer | Cancer |
| | October 24 | November 13 | Scorpio | Scorpio |
| Venus | October 3 | November 14 | Scorpio | Libra |
| Mars | None | | | |
| Jupiter | November 11, 2025 | March 11, 2026 | Cancer | Cancer |
| | December 13, 2026 | April 13, 2027 | Leo | Leo |
| Saturn | July 26 | December 10 | Aries | Aries |
| Uranus | September 6, 2025 | February 4, 2026 | Gemini | Taurus |
| | September 10, 2026 | February 8, 2027 | Gemini | Gemini |
| Neptune | July 7 | December 12 | Aries | Aries |
| Pluto | May 6 | October 16 | Aquarius | Aquarius |
| Chiron | July 30, 2025 | January 2, 2026 | Aries | Aries |
| | August 3, 2026 | January 6, 2027 | Taurus | Aries |

# 2027

| PLANET | IN DATE | OUT DATE | ZODIAC IN | ZODIAC OUT |
|--------|---------|----------|-----------|------------|
| Mercury | February 9 | March 3 | Pisces | Aquarius |
| | June 10 | July 4 | Cancer | Gemini |
| | October 7 | October 28 | Scorpio | Libra |
| Venus | None | | | |
| Mars | January 10 | April 1 | Virgo | Leo |
| Jupiter | December 13, 2026 | April 13, 2027 | Leo | Leo |
| Saturn | August 9 | December 24 | Aries | Aries |
| Uranus | September 10, 2026 | February 8, 2027 | Gemini | Gemini |
| | September 15, 2027 | February 12, 2028 | Gemini | Gemini |
| Neptune | July 9 | September 15 | Aries | Aries |
| Pluto | May 8 | October 18 | Aquarius | Aquarius |
| Chiron | August 3, 2026 | January 6, 2027 | Taurus | Aries |
| | August 8, 2027 | January 10, 2028 | Taurus | Taurus |

# 2028

| PLANET | IN DATE | OUT DATE | ZODIAC IN | ZODIAC OUT |
|--------|---------|----------|-----------|------------|
| Mercury | January 24 | February 14 | Aquarius | Aquarius |
| | May 21 | June 14 | Gemini | Gemini |
| | September 19 | October 11 | Libra | Libra |
| Venus | May 10 | June 22 | Gemini | Gemini |
| Mars | None | | | |
| Jupiter | January 12 | May 13 | Virgo | Virgo |
| Saturn | August 22, 2028 | January 25, 2029 | Taurus | Taurus |
| Uranus | September 15, 2027 | February 12, 2028 | Gemini | Gemini |
| | September 19, 2028 | February 16, 2029 | Gemini | Gemini |
| Neptune | July 11 | December 16 | Aries | Aries |
| Pluto | May 9 | October 19 | Aquarius | Aquarius |
| Chiron | August 8, 2027 | January 10, 2028 | Taurus | Taurus |
| | August 11, 2028 | January 13, 2029 | Taurus | Taurus |

# 2029

| PLANET | IN DATE | OUT DATE | ZODIAC IN | ZODIAC OUT |
|--------|---------|----------|-----------|------------|
| Mercury | January 7 | January 27 | Aquarius | Capricorn |
| | May 1 | May 25 | Taurus | Taurus |
| | September 2 | September 25 | Libra | Virgo |
| | December 22, 2029 | January 11, 2030 | Capricorn | Capricorn |
| Venus | December 16, 2029 | January 26, 2030 | Capricorn | Capricorn |
| Mars | February 14 | May 5 | Libra | Virgo |
| Jupiter | February 10 | June 13 | Libra | Libra |
| Saturn | August 22, 2028 | January 25, 2029 | Taurus | Taurus |
| | September 6, 2029 | January 19, 2030 | Taurus | Taurus |
| Uranus | September 19, 2028 | February 16, 2029 | Gemini | Gemini |
| | September 23, 2029 | February 20, 2030 | Gemini | Gemini |
| Neptune | July 14 | December 19 | Aries | Aries |
| Pluto | May 11 | October 21 | Aquarius | Aquarius |
| Chiron | August 11, 2028 | January 13, 2029 | Taurus | Taurus |
| | August 16, 2029 | January 17, 2030 | Taurus | Taurus |

# 2030

| PLANET | IN DATE | OUT DATE | ZODIAC IN | ZODIAC OUT |
|---|---|---|---|---|
| Mercury | December 22, 2029 | January 11, 2030 | Capricorn | Capricorn |
|  | April 13 | May 6 | Taurus | Aries |
|  | August 16 | September 8 | Virgo | Virgo |
|  | December 6 | December 25 | Capricorn | Sagittarius |
| Venus | December 16, 2029 | January 26, 2030 | Capricorn | Capricorn |
| Mars | None |  |  |  |
| Jupiter | March 13 | July 15 | Scorpio | Scorpio |
| Saturn | September 6, 2029 | January 19, 2030 | Taurus | Taurus |
|  | September 20, 2030 | February 2, 2031 | Gemini | Gemini |
| Uranus | September 23, 2029 | February 20, 2030 | Gemini | Gemini |
|  | September 28, 2030 | February 25, 2031 | Gemini | Gemini |
| Neptune | July 16 | December 21 | Aries | Aries |
| Pluto | May 12 | October 23 | Aquarius | Aquarius |
| Chiron | August 16, 2029 | January 17, 2030 | Taurus | Taurus |
|  | August 21, 2030 | January 21, 2031 | Taurus | Taurus |

# SECTION IV

## RESOURCES

# GLOSSARY

**Aspect:** The angle two planets are separated by in an astrological chart.

**Birth Chart:** What the planets looked like in the astrological sky the second you were born, plotted out on a circular chart that includes the placement of each planet in each zodiac sign.

**Celestial Body:** Anything that moves through the sky in orbit.

**Chiron:** Astrologically, Chiron is a minor planet in the outer solar system between Saturn and Uranus. Scientifically, it's classified as both a comet and a minor planet.

**Collective Planets:** Uranus, Neptune, and Pluto are collective planets, meaning they represent the overall views of society. They are also known as transpersonal or generational.

**Conjunction:** When two planets are fewer than 10 degrees apart.

**Degrees:** Astrological charts are broken down into 360 degrees, marking each segment of movement around the sky. Each zodiac sign occupies 30 degrees. In astrological charts, the planets are notated with what degree they fall into in each zodiac sign.

**Direct:** Also called *prograde*. This is when a planet is moving east to west, or in a right-to-left direction through the sky.

**Ecliptic:** This is the path the sun takes through the sky and the constellations from the perspective of Earth. It runs through the middle of the zodiac.

**Ephemeris:** A book of charts that shows all the positions of all the planets (plus the sun and moon) for the next year. It also contains eclipse information and astrological influence information. It's similar to the *Farmer's Almanac*, but for astronomy and astrology.

**Event Chart:** The astrological chart written up for a specific event in history, like Abraham Lincoln's assassination or your first day of college.

**House:** Astrological charts are broken up into 12 houses, each representing a different part of your life, like relationships or career.

**Luminaries:** The sun and moon.

**Moon Sign:** The zodiac sign where the moon was the day you were born.

**Natal:** At the time of birth. If you have a natal retrograde in your birth chart, it means a planet was retrograde when you were born.

**Nodes:** Mathematical points marking the spot in the sky where the sun and moon pass one another as seen from Earth.

**Opposition:** When two planets are 180 degrees apart.

**Personal Planets:** In astrology, the sun, moon, Mercury, Venus, and Mars are considered personal planets. They represent the core of your personality and character as an individual.

**Transit:** The name for a planet's movement across the sky.

**Retrograde:** This is when a planet appears to be moving in the opposite direction to the one it typically goes—a left-to-right motion.

**Return:** Returns are different for everyone. They happen when a planet goes back to the same sign and degree it was in on the day you were born.

**Rising Sign:** Also called "the ascendant," this zodiac sign would have been located on the eastern horizon on the day you were born.

**Rx, ℞:** This is an abbreviation for the word "retrograde." You'll normally see it on a birth chart if someone had a planet retrograde when they were born.

**Sect:** Your sect indicates whether you were born during the day (diurnal) or in the evening (nocturnal).

**Sextile:** Planets that are 60 degrees apart.

**Shadow Period:** A period of time just before or after a planetary retrograde.

**Social Planets:** Jupiter and Saturn are considered social planets. They represent how we personally interact with the world at large.

**Squares:** Planets that are 90 degrees apart.

**Station:** When a planet turns retrograde or direct.

**Sun Sign:** Your primary astrological sign, denoted by where the sun was when you were born.

**Trine:** A positioning in which planets are 120 degrees apart.

**Zodiac:** A 12-section chart that represents the constellations the sun, moon, and planets move through as viewed from Earth.

# Websites

Aquarius Papers, aquariuspapers.com. One of the longest-running astrology blogs on the internet.

Astrodienst, astro.com. A monthly newsletter and blog, with a quick glance at what all the planets are doing astrologically in the solar system at any given time.

Astrolabe, alabe.com. A website selling astrology software and other astrology products. You can also generate a free birth chart here.

Astrology.com. An online publication covering all things astrology.

Astrology Hub, astrologyhub.com. A website offering a blog from trusted astrologers, a podcast, classes, events, and a membership program connecting astrologers with astrology fans.

Astrology Zone, astrologyzone.com. A popular website for generating birth charts as well as getting daily and monthly horoscopes.

Astro-Seek, astro-seek.com. An informational astrological website that also allows users to create a profile to find their AstroTwin, or someone with the same birthday.

Café Astrology, cafeastrology.com. This web publication is all about astrology and is one of the most popular websites for free birth charts.

The Hoodwitch, thehoodwitch.com. The website and blog of popular Seattle-based mystic Bri Luna.

# Books

*Astrology: Using the Wisdom of the Stars in Your Everyday Life* by Carole Taylor

*Chiron and the Healing Journey* by Melanie Reinhart

*The Contemporary Astrologer's Handbook* by Sue Tompkins

*Cosmos and Psyche: Intimations of a New World View* by Richard Tarnas

*Eclipses: Predicting World Events & Personal Transformation* by Celeste Teal

*Karmic Astrology: Retrogrades and Reincarnation* by Martin Schulman

*A New Look at Mercury Retrograde* by Robert Wilkinson

*The Only Astrology Book You'll Ever Need* by Joanna Martine Woolfolk

*Saturn: Spiritual Master, Spiritual Friend* by Robert Wilkinson

*The Signs* by Carolyne Faulkner

*The Stars Within You* by Juliana McCarthy

*The Magic of Venus: Friendships, Soulmates, and Twin Flames* by Robert Wilkinson

# Podcasts

*Allegedly Astrology*. A weekly podcast connecting pop culture, history, and astrology.

*The Astrology Hub Podcast*. Featuring astrological guidance from guest astrologers.

*Your Astrology and Horoscope Forecast with Kelli Fox*. Discussing weekly and monthly astrology forecasts, astrological weather, and horoscopes.

*Astrology of the Week Ahead*. Weekly cosmic guidance with astrologer host Chani Nicholas.

*The Astrology Podcast*. Astrologer Chris Brennan takes listeners through the history and philosophy of astrology.

*The Daily Witch*. A news podcast about all things witchy, with a dedicated astrologer.

*Intuitive Connection*. All about being an empath and connecting with spiritual intuition.

*The Stellium Astrology Podcast*. Deep dives into various styles of astrology.

# Apps

Astro Future. Offers multiple types of astrological charts and detailed horoscopes.

AstroStyle. An app providing detailed horoscopes for you and those you love.

Co-Star. An app that offers the ability to compare your personalized astrology reports with your friends' personalized astrology reports.

Labyrinthos. An app for learning how to read tarot cards.

TimePassages. Free daily horoscopes and personalized astrology readings.

# Schools

Avalon School of Astrology, avalonastrology.com

Academy of AstroPsychology, AstroPsychology.org

Astrology University, astrologyuniversity.com

The Faculty of Astrological Studies, astrology.org.uk

Kepler College, keplercollege.org

Midwest School of Astrology, midwestschoolofastrology.com

# Organizations

American Federation of Astrologers, astrologers.com

Astrological Association, astrologicalassociation.com

International Society for Astrological Research, isarastrology.org

National Council for Geocosmic Research, geocosmic.org

Organization for Professional Astrology, opaastrology.org

# Astrologers from This Book

Brian Allemana, Soulrise Astrology, soulriseastrology.com (he/him)

KJ Atlas, kjatlas.com (she/her)

Madeline Gerwick, Polaris Business Guides, polarisbusinessguides.com (she/her)

Andi Javor, Mystic Sandwich, mysticsandwich.com (she/her)

Charly King, Astrologer and Radio Host, bobandsheri.com/author/charlyk (she/her)

Angelica Kurtz, Astro Obscura, astroobscura.com (she/her)

Susan Levitt, susanlevitt.com (she/her)

Julia Mihas, Astrology & Life Coaching, juliamihas.com (she/her)

Deborah Norton, Deborah Norton Astrology, deborahnorton.com (she/her)

Rowan Oliver, StarScribe Astrology, rowastrology.com (they/them)

Mashi Salomon, Light and Lavender, https://www.facebook.com/p/Light-and-Lavender-Intuitive-Energy-Services-100070671261693 (she/her)

Robert Wilkinson, Aquarius Papers, aquariuspapers.com (he/him)

# ABOUT THE AUTHOR

Jennifer Billock is a freelance writer, author, eclectic witch, and fortune teller. She loves blending witchcraft and writing, often with a focus on food or astrology. Jennifer is a Leo and has the naturally outsized and quirky personality to match.

Jennifer has her MS in journalism from Roosevelt University with undergraduate degrees from Columbia College Chicago and the College of Lake County. In a former life, she was a high school choir teacher and an award-winning vocalist. Her hobbies include traveling, reading, petting every animal, and anything outdoors. She also coaches young writers on every aspect of the freelance writing business.